THE SELF AND THE OBJECT WORLD

Journal of the American Psychoanalytic Association
Monograph Series Number Two

THE SELF AND
THE OBJECT WORLD

EDITH JACOBSON, M.D.

International Universities Press, Inc.

NEW YORK   NEW YORK

Contents

Part I

Early Infantile, Preoedipal, and Oedipal Phases

Part II

Superego Formation and the Period of Latency

Foreword

THE JOURNAL of the American Psychoanalytic Association considers itself most fortunate in being able to sponsor the publication of this contribution as the second in its Monograph series.

Dr. Jacobson's studies on psychotic depression were inextricably interwoven with an examination of the fate of the child's relationship to the primary love object and inevitably led to a study of the earliest stages in psychic development. This culminated in a most provocative paper, "The Self and the Object World," published in 1954. Many ideas in that paper were further amplified and elaborated on in subsequent works: thus this Monograph is both a summary and an extension of these contributions. However, it is not merely an expanded version of "The Self and the Object World," nor is its scope limited to the subject matter of its title. In its greater comprehensiveness it offers a systematic frame of reference for a psychoanalytic genetic psychology which encompasses the early phases of psychic development, latency, adolescence, and adulthood. Superb accounts of the adolescent phase of development as well as of the role of the ego and superego in guilt and shame are welcome additions to the understanding of these complicated problems.

Most illuminating are Dr. Jacobson's discussions of ego

goals and ego ideal, of the precursors of the superego, and of the factors which eventually lead to the formation of this psychic structure, unique to man. In doing so, she emphasizes the influence of ego maturation upon the development of the superego, calling attention to the reciprocal interplay of forces which eventuates in the formation of particular psychic structures. The author is especially aware of such interaction and of the multidimensional aspects and the genetic continuity of psychic life. She repeatedly demonstrates that no single event in psychic development remains uninfluenced by any other one, and all of them must be integrated. Thus she does not fall prey to the too common error of exaggerating the importance of one particular aspect of development.

In discussing the different stages of psychosexual development, the author examines, reviews, and amplifies many controversial subjects, such as the concepts of identity, infantile orality, and narcissism. The differentiations between ego, self, and self representations are explained with special clarity. Concepts of undifferentiated drive energy, the undifferentiated ego-id and their gradual emergence into functioning psychic structures, are incorporated into a conceptual scheme which illuminates our understanding of many obscure clinical phenomena. The numerous theoretical formulations are bound to strike a responsive note because, in the best tradition of classic psychoanalytic contributions, they are firmly rooted in rich clinical experience.

In her disagreement with other contributors to this field of inquiry, she offers alternative views. Those of us who have had the good fortune to read the manuscript were impressed by the richness of the ideas in this Monograph, which we feel certain will be frequently reread and studied in order to gain a full appreciation of its many implications.

THE EDITORS

Author's Note

I wish to express my warmest gratitude to Dr. John Frosch and to the Editorial Board for encouraging me to write this book. I am especially grateful to Dr. Max Schur for his thorough study and his very helpful discussion of this volume with me. I also want to extend my sincere thanks to Dr. Nathaniel Ross and to Mrs. Lottie Newman for their valuable editorial assistance, and to Miss Paula Gross and Miss Mona M. Karff for their tireless work in preparing the manuscript.

Introduction

In RECENT YEARS, psychoanalysts have paid increasing attention to the fascinating problem of identity. Of course, a fruit-
ful discussion of this problem presupposes precise definitions
of such terms as *self, ego,* and *identity* or *ego identity,* which
are indispensable for constructive analytic approaches to this
and many related questions. Whereas Hartmann (1950) introduced and carefully defined the distinction between the concepts of ego, self, and self representations, there exists no such
generally accepted psychoanalytic definition of the concept
of identity. In fact, the authors who have lately explored
this subject attach quite different meanings to these terms
and consequently arrive at seemingly different conclusions.[1]

In the context of several studies published during the past
decade (1953b, 1954a, 1954b, 1959), I have discussed different
aspects of self awareness, identity, and certain disturbances
in the feeling of identity.

Comparing my ideas with those expressed in recent papers
and books on this subject, I have discovered considerable

[1] As far as I know, the term identity has been introduced into the psychoanalytic literature by Victor Tausk in his brilliant paper on the "influencing
machine" (1919). In this article he examines how the child discovers objects
and his self; he asserts that man, in his struggle for survival, must throughout
life constantly find and experience himself anew (p. 22).

differences of opinion, which have stimulated my own thinking and caused me to expand and reorganize my earlier paper on "The Self and the Object World" (1954a) into this volume bearing the same title.

In my brief introduction to the original study I indicated what I may here re-emphasize. The rising interest in the problem of identity is probably caused by the widening scope of psychoanalysis and the growing number of borderline or even psychotic patients who call on the psychoanalyst for help. In such patients, we can observe processes of regression that lead to a grave deterioration of object relations and of superego and ego functions, with dissolution of those essential identifications on which the experience of our personal identity is founded.

The treatment and supervision of such cases and the analysis of severely narcissistic types of neuroses have convinced me that the problems discussed in this volume and the perspectives from which I approached them are eminently important for the clinical and theoretical understanding of these patients. For this reason, I decided to make frequent references to the pathology of psychoses.

The additional parts of this volume offer a critical review of the literature on identity and discuss the mutual influences which the development of identity, the vicissitudes of object relations and identifications, and the establishment of the ego-superego systems exercise on each other. I have also added a further discussion of the infantile period of superego formation and of the complex developmental processes during the adolescent period which are so significant for identity formation and the ultimate regulation of self esteem.

The necessity of dealing with those aspects of the problem which seemed to me most essential to the hypotheses put forth in this volume compelled me to disregard many significant observational, clinical, and theoretical studies on infantile and adolescent development, even though they are highly pertinent to the subjects which will be discussed. On the other hand, I have decided to take issue with Bowlby's controversial new theories, not only because they touch directly on matters with which this volume is concerned, but primarily because they also point up misunderstandings which may in part be caused by our failure more carefully to re-examine and redefine concepts, such as those of infantile orality and infantile narcissism, in terms of our current knowledge of the earliest stages in the development of the ego.

I realize, of course, that I may not have been as successful as I might wish in integrating new material with an essay written ten years ago. In rereading my first paper I was surprised to note how far the focus of my interest has shifted and how my own thinking has imperceptibly changed during these years. Thus, the present volume shows inevitable incongruities and a regrettable lack of uniformity. In spite of these and other shortcomings, I hope that I have been able to clarify those points which I regard as essential, and to make a modest contribution to the psychoanalysis of normal development processes during childhood and adolescence.

Part I

Early Infantile, Preoedipal, and Oedipal Phases

1

Narcissism, Masochism, and the Concepts of Self and Self Representations

In my brief introduction to this volume I indicated that I intend to scrutinize not only the interrelating development of object relations, identifications, and the feeling of identity, but also the interplay between their vicissitudes and the building up of the ego and superego. My investigation will begin with a review of our psychoanalytic concepts of primary and secondary narcissism and masochism.

The concept of narcissism was introduced by Freud (1914) in his paper "On Narcissism: An Introduction." Freud's point of departure in this paper was the megalomanic symptoms in schizophrenics which, he said,

> . . . doubtless come into being at the expense of the object-libido. The libido withdrawn from the outer world has been directed on to the ego, giving rise to a state which we may call narcissism.
> [Freud concluded that] the narcissism which arises when libidinal cathexes are called in away from external objects must be conceived of as a secondary form, superimposed upon a primary one that is obscured by manifold influences [p. 32].

He commented on the "reciprocity between ego-libido and object-libido" and contrasted the narcissistic condition of the schizophrenic with the yielding up of the "whole personality

[3]

in favour of object-cathexis" (p. 33) in the state of being in love.

Freud found his concept of a primary infantile narcissism reinforced by the signs of megalomanic attitudes in primitives and in the child:

> [their] over-estimation of the power of wishes and mental processes, the 'omnipotence of thoughts', a belief in the magic virtue of words, and a method of dealing with the outer world—the art of 'magic'—which appears to be a logical application of these grandiose premises [p. 32].

In *The Ego and the Id* (1923), Freud developed his concept of narcissism further:

> At the very beginning all the libido is accumulated in the id, while the ego is still in a process of formation or far from robust. Part of this libido is sent out by the id into erotic object-cathexes, whereupon the ego, now growing stronger, attempts to obtain possession of this object-libido and to force itself upon the id as a love-object. The narcissism of the ego is thus seen to be secondary, acquired by the withdrawal of the libido from objects [p. 65].

Freud's ideas on primary narcissism and on the development of secondary narcissism were significantly supplemented by his proposition of parallel vicissitudes of the death instincts. In *Beyond the Pleasure Principle* (1920) he suggested that

> . . . sadism is properly a death instinct which is driven apart from the ego by the influence of the narcissistic libido, so that it becomes manifest only in reference to the object [p. 60].

In *An Outline of Psychoanalysis* Freud (1940) wrote:

> We may picture an initial state of things by supposing that the whole available energy of Eros, to which we shall

[4]

henceforward give the name of *libido,* is present in the as yet undifferentiated ego-id[1] and serves to neutralize the destructive impulses which are simultaneously present. (There is no term analogous to "libido" for describing the energy of the destructive instinct.) [p. 22].

In "The Economic Problem of Masochism" Freud (1924) said, furthermore, that

. . . under certain conditions the sadism or destructive instinct which has been directed outwards can be introjected, turned inward again, regressing in this way to its earlier condition. It then provides that secondary masochism which supplements the original one [p. 261].

Freud then described the erotogenic masochism as the original, primary one which was never directed outward but remained in the organism, bound down by libido.

The erotogenic type of masochism passes through all the developmental stages of the libido, and from them it takes the changing shapes it wears in the life of the mind [p. 261].

Freud found that the severe masochistic trends sometimes encountered in neuroses and psychoses, especially in melancholia, supported his assumption of a primary masochism and could be explained by it. "What is now holding sway in the super-ego," he said in *The Ego and the Id* (1923), "is, as it were, a pure culture of the death instinct, and in fact it often enough succeeds in driving the ego into death" (p. 77).

In view of Freud's propositions, it seems advisable to combine the discussion of narcissism with that of masochism. I shall first concentrate on the meaning of Freud's concepts of

[1] This thought has been elaborated by Hartmann (1939) and by Hartmann, Kris, and Loewenstein (1946).

primary narcissism and primary masochism. His formulations cited above are indeed rather ambiguous. They partly refer only to the simultaneous *presence* of libidinal and aggressive forces in the undifferentiated "psychosomatic" matrix which I shall henceforth call the *primal psychophysiological self*.[2] But the terms "narcissism" and "masochism" imply that originally the drives are actually turned toward, i.e., aimed at discharge on, this primal self. To be sure, the latter idea is the basis of Freud's conception of the death instinct. The original investment of the primal self with aggressive forces is considered a potential danger to the self, warded off by the protective presence of libido. I believe that these conceptions are quite puzzling and require elucidation.

Regarding the advance in psychic organization which takes place after structural differentiation and establishment of self and object representations have been established, we know fairly well, at least practically, what we mean by the turning of libido or aggression toward the self. People who

2 The term "self," which was introduced by Hartmann (1950), will, in agreement with him, be employed as referring to the whole person of an individual, including his body and body parts as well as his psychic organization and its parts. As the title of this volume indicates, the "self" is an auxiliary descriptive term, which points to the person as a subject in distinction from the surrounding world of objects. In order to clarify what I mean, I shall employ terms such a person's "body self" or his "physical self" or his "psychophysiological self" or his "mental self" or "psychic self." To distinguish the concept "self" from its ordinary usage, I have omitted the customary hyphenation of all compound nouns with self.

Rapaport (1956) criticized me for supposedly equating the "self" with the "self representations," a metapsychological concept which will be defined later. Although I discriminated quite carefully between these concepts, it is true that for semantic reasons I occasionally referred to the self or the objects when it seemed to be clear that I actually meant their psychic representations. In this volume I shall make special efforts to avoid confusing terminological inaccuracies. However, this is not always possible. It may be recalled that Freud, too, often briefly referred to objects when he clearly meant their psychic representations.

display narcissistic or masochistic sexual or social behavior document clearly enough the tendency to withdraw object cathexis and to make their own persons the objects of either love, admiration, and libidinal gratification, or of hate, depreciation, and destructiveness. But what precisely is the meaning of narcissism and masochism in the primitive psychic organization prior to the child's discovery of his own self and of the object world? To obtain an answer, we obviously must turn to a study of the drive manifestations of the infant and try to give a precise metapsychological description of his state and behavior.

Between the brief feeding periods the infant spends most of the time either in a sleeping or in a half-awake, dozing state of passivity with as yet little expression of even primitive affects or of perceptive and motor functions. Sleep is the state which we are accustomed to designate as a truly narcissistic situation.

In "A Metapsychological Supplement to the Theory of Dreams" (1917a), Freud said:

> Somatically, sleep is an act which reproduces intra-uterine existence, fulfilling the conditions of repose, warmth and absence of stimulus; indeed, in sleeping, many people resume the foetal position. The feature characterizing the mind of a sleeping person is an almost complete withdrawal from the surrounding world and the cessation of all interest in it [pp. 137-138].
> [And, further on:] The narcissism of sleep does indeed signify the withdrawal of cathexis from all ideas of objects, both from the unconscious and the preconscious parts of them [p. 140].

Quite in accord with Freud's description, we may visualize the original psychoeconomic state, the state that still prevails in the early infantile sleeping, dozing, passive situation, as a condition of diffuse dispersion of instinctual forces within the whole undifferentiated psychophysiological self. But considering the meaning of the terms "narcissism" and "masochism," the interesting question arises: by which avenues is psychic energy discharged during such a state?

Some authors occasionally speak of discharge either outward or inward, but without elaborating on what they mean. To be sure, we do not yet have sufficient insight into the connections between drive-discharge phenomena and concomitant physiological processes to understand the precise meaning of such concepts. What we know is, very vaguely, that discharge to the outside involves the perceptive and motor apparatus and results in affectomotor phenomena and motor actions, whereas discharge toward the inside entails physiological processes inducing functional changes chiefly in the inner body organs. However, despite the admitted vagueness of these concepts, the distinction of discharge to the inside or outside appears to be highly relevant for the understanding of the early infantile drive qualities and of the earliest forerunners of affective and ideational life.

In all likelihood, the limited early infantile contact with the outside world and its stimuli keeps the general level of tension in the psychic apparatus comparatively low; moreover, the cathexis of the body organs probably still outweighs that of the periphery, i.e., of the perceptive and, in particular, of the motor apparatus. In this way, a continuous, "silent" discharge of small amounts of psychic energy may occur during the periods between feedings mainly through "inside" physiological channels.[3]

3 Of course, the significant work by Fisher and his collaborators (1954, 1957, 1959), and other researchers on the psychic activity during the sleeping state will eventually require careful reformulations of the psychophysiological and psychoeconomic situation of the infant as well as the adult during sleep.

Thus, the psychoeconomic condition and the type of discharge characteristic of the sleeping or dozing infant and of the sleeping state in general, and evidently also of pathological states of deep, so-called narcissistic regression, suggest that physiological discharge toward the inside, i.e., on the self, may be regarded as the earliest infantile form of drive discharge.

As the embryonal movements show, even before birth the embryo is able to discharge drive energy also through motor channels. At birth, however, a drastic readjustment takes place, enforced by the environmental changes. The first signs of life in the newborn—his cry, and furthermore the characteristic behavior displayed before, during, and after feeding and in his excretory functions—are indeed beginning manifestations of prepatterned affectomotor discharge processes in response to stimulations not only from within but from without.

Of course, the infant, though gaining stimulation and gratification from an "object"—the mother—as well as from his own body, is as yet unaware of anything but pleasurable or unpleasurable sensations. In view of this, we are entitled to describe his drive manifestations, in general, as "narcissistic." But it is of relevance to realize that they represent drive discharge not only toward the inside, "on the self," but that from birth onward the infant has at his disposal biologically predetermined, though limited, channels for discharge to the outside. The latter is the precursor of object-directed discharge.

My emphasis on the distinction between discharge to the inside and to the outside will prove to be useful for the study of the vicissitudes of the self-directed and of the object-directed libidinal and aggressive drive-discharge processes, and of their influence on affective, ideational, and functional

[9]

development. I shall presently scrutinize the connection between discharge to the inside and to the outside and the affective and instinctual manifestations of the infant's behavior.

In Chapter VI of *The Interpretation of Dreams,* Freud (1900) makes the following statement:

"I am compelled—for other reasons—to picture the release of affects as a centrifugal process directed towards the interior of the body and analogous to the processes of motor and secretory innervation. Now just as in the state of sleep the sending out of motor impulses towards the external world appears to be suspended, so it may be that the centrifugal calling-up of affects by unconscious thinking may become more difficult during sleep" [pp. 467-468].

Freud's (1915) later definition of affects in "The Unconscious" adheres to some extent to this idea. It is noteworthy that his remarks characterize affective discharge as "resulting in an (internal) alteration of the subject's own body" (p. 111), but at the same time as a centrifugal process whose liberation is precluded by the state of sleep in the same way as is the discharge of motor impulses. At first sight, this statement may appear puzzling or even contradictory. Its meaning becomes perfectly clear when we realize that in this context "centrifugal" obviously refers to "outside the mental apparatus." Relinquishing the use of the term centrifugal as possibly confusing, I prefer simply to state that in contradistinction to the "silent," predominantly psychophysiological discharge of the embryo or newborn or during sleep, the emotions of the adult find expression not only in secretory, circulatory, respiratory phenomena indicative of physiological discharge toward the inside, but also in patterned motor phenomena and in the inner perceptions which we call feelings, i.e., in manifestations of discharge toward the outside.

[10]

Thus we may surmise that the inhibition of affects during the state of sleep might be accomplished by their temporary and partial regressive retransformation into silent physiological and hallucinatory visual discharge.

We may now return to my previous statements suggesting that psychic life originates in physiological processes which are independent of external sensory stimulations. From birth on, however, the discharge processes expand with the opening up of biologically predetermined and preferred pathways for discharge in response to external stimulation. They lead at first only to primitive, patterned motor, species-specific (instinctive) reactions, and to pleasurable or unpleasurable sensory experiences which cannot yet be called feelings. Evidently these phenomena are no more than genetic forerunners of the emotional and thought processes and of the complex functional activities whose development sets in with the beginning of ego formation. In fact, during the first infantile stages, the predominant expression of the child's emotional and fantasy life is still "psychophysiological," the so-called "affective organ language" which encompasses, however, not only the "silent" inner physiological processes emphasized above but also visible vasomotor and secretory phenomena and manifestations in the realm of oral and excretory functions. I may point out that this affective organ language survives, to some extent, even in the emotional life of normal adults in anxiety states and in other manifestations of "resomatization" of affects (Schur, 1955).

The foregoing considerations were intended to underline the correlation of the original psychoeconomic state and the earliest type of drive discharge within the self to the psychophysiological forerunners of adult affective and ideational expression. The value of such considerations is proved by

[11]

observations on patients with psychosomatic diseases or psychotic disorders, which confirm these correlations.

These two groups of disorders show what we call, albeit somewhat imprecisely, signs of severe narcissistic regression. With regard to psychosomatic patients we may, in the light of my proposition, speak of a pathological partial retransformation of ideational and emotional into somatic, physiological expressions, which are then perceived only as painful body sensations (Schur, 1955). In psychoses, the depressed or catatonic stuporous states appear to be pathological versions of the infant's dozing states. To be sure, there are significant differences between the psychic economy and the drive qualities in such pathological, regressive states and the original conditions of which they are reminiscent. These disorders show convincing evidence of destructive and self-destructive processes, not only psychological but also physiological, of which we find no signs in the normal state of sleep and in the healthy, early infantile childhood state. Quite the contrary: physiologically and psychologically the sleeping state has a recuperative function, and the embryonal state serves the psychophysiological growth of the organism.

These differences underscore the misunderstanding which may result from the use of the term "narcissistic regression" with regard to pathological processes of such a destructive or self-destructive nature. We must not forget that the concept of narcissism preceded Freud's introduction of a dual drive theory. And being extremely useful, this concept and the term asserted themselves despite the fact that they do not bear reference to the aggressive drives.[4] For reasons we shall soon understand, Freud's attempts to modify the con-

---

[4] Thus Abraham (1924) in his discussion of psychotic depression spoke of "a positive and a negative narcissism" (p. 456) in his description of the melancholic's self love and self hatred.

cept of narcissism and to relate it to his new propositions did not clarify this issue quite satisfactorily.

But before discussing how this concept can be adapted to a dual drive theory and to the structural concepts, we must face the question whether my previous psychoeconomic considerations make it advisable at all to adhere to the concept of a primary masochism, i.e., of a death instinct. The assumption that those unobservable, inner psychophysiological discharge processes in the sleeping or dozing infant may also guarantee a harmless, diffuse discharge of small amounts of aggressive energy certainly presents a difficult problem.

Freud tried to resolve it by assuming that in the primary narcissistic-masochistic state the presence of life instincts prevents self destruction. But how can this occur? We understand that fusions between libido and aggression render the destructive drives harmless. This process, however, develops at a much later infantile period; it is connected with the partial neutralization of the drives.

Consequently we may wonder whether the observable facts might not be explained more readily by the assumption that, at the very beginning of life, the instinctual energy is still in an undifferentiated state; and that from birth on it develops into two kinds of psychic drives with different qualities under the influence of external stimulations, of psychic growth and the opening up and increasing maturation of pathways for outside discharge.[5] Looking for confirmation of this hypothesis, I find it noteworthy that during infancy and even in early childhood it is not easy to discern the aggressive and libidinal qualities in the child's instinctual and emotional manifestations, and that such affective phe-

[5] Cf. Fenichel (1945, p. 58). This idea would not imply, however, that the drive qualities are determined only by the specific avenues for discharge.

[13]

nomena as anxiety and rage still appear to be closely interwoven.

While such a conception may be reminiscent of the frustration-aggression theory, it should be noted that the transformation of undifferentiated psychophysiological energy into two qualitatively different kinds of psychic drives is here regarded as psychobiologically predetermined and as promoted by internal maturational factors as well as by external stimuli.

The idea also calls to mind Freud's interesting remarks in *The Ego and the Id* (1923), to the effect that an amount of "neutral [*indifferente*] displaceable energy" (p. 62) is apt to join forces with either libido or aggression. Freud's significant assumption of desexualized energy, which however is supposed "to be active alike in the ego and in the id" (p. 63), might be even more convincing if it referred not to desexualized but to originally undifferentiated drive energy in the whole primal psychophysiological self. If we accept this hypothesis, we must adjust our thinking to the following conceptions:

To summarize once more, we may visualize an initial psychoeconomic state, characterized by a low level of tension and by a general, diffuse dispersion of as yet undifferentiated psychophysiological energy within the primal, structurally also undifferentiated self. Under the influence of both, of intrinsic factors and of external stimuli, the undifferentiated forces would then begin to develop into the libidinal and aggressive psychic drives with which the id is endowed. During the embryonal and also predominantly during the earliest infantile stage, most of this undifferentiated energy of the primal self is diffusely discharged in small amounts on the inside at first exclusively through physiological channels. But after birth the pregenital erogenous zones and, to an increasing degree, the whole sensory and motor systems, the "primary autonomous" core of the future ego, become periodically hypercathected; processes of drive discharge toward the outside begin to develop, which become observable in pregenital (sexual and aggressive) activity and in biologically prepatterned, primitive affectomotor and instinctive reflex motor reactions, easily recognizable as the forerunners of feeling, thinking, and of motor and other ego functions. In the course of structural differentiation the libidinal and aggressive drives would undergo processes of fusion and partial neutralization. These neutralized drives, together with part of the libidinal and aggressive drives, would become vested in the new systems, the ego and the superego, and could be utilized for the building up of emotional and thought processes and the corresponding ego and superego functions.

Should these propositions be valid, they would compel us to dispose of the concept of primary masochism, i.e., of Freud's death instinct theory. Being rather speculative, the latter has, in any event, found less acceptance than the simpler dual drive theory in terms of two basic drives, libido and aggression. In view of my assumption that the libidinal and the aggressive drives develop from undifferentiated drive energy, I suggested, in my previous paper on "The Self and the Object World" (1954a, p. 83) that we also dispense with the concept of primary narcissism. At the present time, however, it seems to me that it is still a very useful term for the earliest infantile period, preceding the development of self and object images, the stage during which the infant is as yet unaware of anything but his own experiences of tension and relief, of frustration and gratification. But we must keep in mind that this term bears no reference to energic and structural differentiation and the corresponding establishment and cathexis of self and object representations. Let us consider the difference between the condition during the earliest developmental stage and states of severe pathological (narcissistic) regression in the light of my hypotheses. We would then have to distinguish processes of *structural* from those of *energic* regression. These would lead not only to deneutralization of the psychic energy of the ego but to partial regressive retransformation of the instinctual forces into primary, undifferentiated energy.[6]

My proposition would also explain a mystery for which the drive-fusion and drive-defusion theory cannot account: the fact that drive fusions appear to result in an absolute prevalence of libidinal drive energy, while drive defusions bring about libidinal impoverishment and absolute predominance of aggressive drive energy.[7] The change of the proportions between libido and aggression, which in such severely regressive processes as the psychoses can lead to actual exhaustion of the libidinal resources of the self (or, possibly, be its result), would be much more understandable if we thought in terms of intermediary stages of retransformation of differentiated into primordial, undifferentiated drive energy.

The afore-stated proposition would furthermore permit us to include once more physiological tension, such as hunger, in the framework of psychoanalytic theory. This has no place at present in our conception of only two drives—libidinal and aggressive. Hunger, once designated by Freud as an ego drive, would then be the expression of such primitive, un-

[6] Possibly this further regressive process may develop as a temporary or lasting result of shock treatment or surgical therapy of psychotics and may account for their therapeutic effects. After such treatments one can actually observe a period of complete absence of libidinal as well as aggressive drive manifestations.

[7] In a personal discussion, years ago, I called Fenichel's attention to this point.

differentiated, psychophysiological drive tensions. Should we be inclined to speculate, the proposition might even explain some of the issues which Freud discussed in the light of his life and death instinct theory. What I have said about psychotic and psychosomatic diseases might be extended to processes of aging and physical decline. All such processes might involve a decrease in the cathexes of the periphery, of perceptive and motor functions, resulting in a rise of the cathexis of the body organs, with concomitant regressive drive defusion to the point of prevalence of destructive drive energy, which must again be discharged through physiological channels in the body.[8]

We are now ready to take up the concepts of secondary narcissism and secondary masochism. I stated above that from the "practical" point of view we know rather well what we mean by narcissism and masochism as they exist in more advanced states of psychic organization. Nevertheless, I must introduce this discussion by stating that here, too, our theoretical concepts and terminology are far from being precise and in accord with modern trends.

From the vantage point of the foregoing considerations, we understand that the development of "secondary narcissism" and "secondary masochism" sets in at the stage of beginning ego formation. In this stage, on the one hand, distinct libidinal and aggressive drive qualities have developed and, on the other, all degrees of fusions between these drives take place. The objects begin to be distinguished

[8] It would also be interesting to compare, from this perspective, the different degrees of regression in psychosomatic diseases and in hysteria. In contrast to the former, which result in a deeply regressive hypercathexis of the inner body organs, hysteria would not only sustain the cathexes of the periphery but even lead to a hypercathexis of the sensory and motor organs at the site of the affection, with partial retransformation of normal affective, ideational, and functional motor discharge into primitive affectomotor and physiological discharge processes finding expression in the hysterical conversion symptoms.

[17]

from each other and from the self, and their different representations in the new system, the ego, gradually become endowed with an enduring libidinal and aggressive cathexis.

As a point of departure for the discussion of this stage, I may repeat part of the quotation from *The Ego and the Id* (1923) where Freud states: "Part of this libido is sent out by the id into erotic object-cathexes, whereupon the ego, now growing stronger, attempts to obtain possession of this object-libido and to force itself upon the id as a love-object. The narcissism of the ego is thus seen to be secondary, acquired by the withdrawal of the libido from objects" (p. 65).

Freud's statement underscores the fact that the development of secondary narcissism is a complex process closely linked up with the structural differentiation and the constitution of the system ego. However, as we begin to think over Freud's formulations, our perplexity sets in; for they are apt to suggest, indeed, that the ego is built up and gains strength by being vested only with narcissistic libido. Our customary terminology confirms this idea. We are accustomed to thinking of secondary narcissism in terms of a cathexis of the ego with narcissistic libido and in general to describe gratifications gained from ego activities simply as "narcissistic gratifications."

The deep well of all object-directed libidinal and aggressive strivings is certainly the id. One of the major achievements of infantile development, however, is undoubtedly also the building up of stable object representations and the establishment of enduring object-libidinal cathexes in the system ego.[9] We appear to be on the horns of a dilemma which, as we shall see, is mainly the result of terminological confusions. They refer to the ambiguous use of the term ego;

9 Accordingly, in *Inhibitions, Symptoms and Anxiety* (1926), Freud himself speaks of sexual impotence as an inhibition of an ego function.

i.e., to the lack of distinction between the ego, which represents a structural mental system, the self, which I defined above, and the self representations. Hartmann (1950), who called attention to this point, suggested the use of the latter term (analogous to object representations) for the unconscious, preconscious, and conscious endopsychic representations of the bodily and mental self in the system ego. I have worked with this concept for years, because I have found it indispensable for the investigation of psychotic disorders.

The meaning of the concepts of the self and self representations, as distinct from that of the ego, becomes clear when we remember that the establishment of the system ego sets in with the discovery of the object world and the growing distinction between it and one's own physical and mental self. From the ever-increasing memory traces of pleasurable and unpleasurable instinctual, emotional, ideational, and functional experiences and of perceptions with which they become associated, images of the love objects as well as those of the bodily and psychic self emerge. Vague and variable at first, they gradually expand and develop into consistent and more or less realistic endopsychic representations of the object world and of the self.

We now understand why Freud's attempt to relate the concept of narcissism to his new structural propositions was not quite successful. Secondary narcissism and masochism are not identical with the libidinal and aggressive endowment of the system ego; it is the mental representations of the self, constituted in the course of ego formation, which become cathected with libido and aggression and turn into objects of love and hate.[10]

[10] Regarding the terminological distinction between the ego, the "self," and the "self representations," it may be of importance to emphasize that the drive cathexes of the latter within the system ego may lead to libidinal or aggressive discharge on the mental or physical self.

Let me now define the concept of self representations more precisely and describe the genetic development of these psychic formations.

As Fenichel (1945) indicated in *The Psychoanalytic Theory of Neurosis,* the image of our self issues from two sources: first, from a direct awareness of our inner experiences, of sensations, of emotional and thought processes, of functional activity; and, second, from indirect self perception and introspection, i.e., from the perception of our bodily and mental self as an object. Since for obvious reasons our capacity for detachment from our own self is at best very limited, our self-cognizant functions contribute only moderately to our conception of the self. Thus the self representations will never be strictly "conceptual." As we shall see, they remain under the influence of our subjective emotional experiences even more than the object representations.[11]

As indicated above, the kernels of the early infantile self images are the memory traces of pleasurable and unpleasurable sensations, which under the influence of autoerotic and of beginning functional activities and of playful general body investigation become associated with body images.

At the start, our image of the self is, like the primitive object image, not a firm unit. Emerging from sensations hardly distinguishable from perceptions of the gratifying part object, it is fused and confused at first with the object images, and is composed of a constantly changing series of self images which reflect mainly the incessant fluctuations of the primitive mental state.[12] We shall discuss the preoedipal develop-

[11] Federn's (1952) concepts of ego feeling and ego experience enphasize this point. But for no good reason, he separates this feeling aspect entirely from the conceptual components of the self representations.

[12] Federn's (1952) assumption of an originally uniform ego feeling is not contradicted by what I said above. As soon as the "I" experience arises, there may be a feeling awareness of the self as a whole, despite the fluidity and variety of self images.

[20]

ment of self and object images further in connection with the problems of identity and identifications.

At present it may suffice to point to the enormous and rather disruptive influences which the processes of infantile denial and repression exert upon the formation of our images of the self and the object world. Since these images arise essentially from the memory traces of pleasurable and unpleasurable experiences and are only gradually linked up with and corrected by the perceptive memories which reflect reality, the cutting out of a considerable sector of unpleasurable memories by infantile repression eliminates a large amount of unacceptable aspects of both the self and the outside world. The defects caused by the work of repression may be filled in by screen elements, by distortions or embellishments produced by the elaborate maneuvers of the ego's defense system. Moreover, to the extent to which the repressed fantasies that have remained cathected in the unconscious can find their way to the surface, they will lend the coloring of past infantile images to the self and object representations.

The universal persistence in women of the unconscious fantasy that their genital is a castrated organ, frequently with simultaneous denial and the development of illusory penis fantasies, may best exemplify how far the impact of infantile emotional experiences prevents us from forming correct body images. This is all the more true with regard to the image of our mental self, which arises only with the growing capacity for self awareness and introspection, i.e., with the capacity for perception, discrimination, and evaluation of our own feelings, thoughts, and actions. These are functions which develop much later than bodily self perception and, though enhanced by superego formation, are in many people only moderately well developed.

But the ubiquitous unconscious fixation, in men as well,

to the fantasy of female castration, also discloses our limited ability to form realistic object representations. They are apt to be colored by our emotions and by past emotional conflicts more than we like to admit. Again, this is especially true for our concepts of the mental characteristics of others. We must consider that our view of the world, and especially of the animate object world, handicapped as it is by the insufficiency of human perception, easily permits distortions by transference of infantile images onto other persons and matters; that it is determined partly by subjective emotional reactions to others' behavior, partly by an empathic understanding founded on primitive affective identifications and often enough on projections. Thus, we can easily understand why there arises such a multiplicity of errors and falsifications.

In any event, with advancing psychosexual and ego development, with the maturation of physical and mental abilities, of emotional and ideational processes and of reality testing, and with increasing capacity for perception and self perception, for judgment and introspection, the images become unified, organized, and integrated into more or less realistic concepts of the object world and of the self.

By a realistic image of the self we mean, first of all, one that correctly mirrors the state and the characteristics, the potentialities and abilities, the assets and the limits of our bodily and mental self: on the one hand, of our appearance, our anatomy, and our physiology; on the other hand, of our ego, our conscious and preconscious feelings and thoughts, wishes, impulses, and attitudes, of our physical and mental functions and behavior. Since ego ideal and superego are part of our mental self, such an image must also correctly depict our preconscious and conscious ideals and scales of value, and the effectiveness—or ineffectiveness—of our self-critical functions. To the extent to which, at any level, the id communicates with the ego or finds access to it, the id, too, is naturally represented in the image of the self.

Whereas all these single specific aspects will have corresponding psychic representations, a concept of their sum total will simultaneously develop; i.e., an awareness of the self as a differentiated but organized entity which "is separate and distinct from one's environment" (Kramer, 1955, p. 47), an entity which has continuity and direction and, to quote Lichtenstein (1961), has "the capacity to remain the same in the midst of change" (p. 193). This awareness will find an emotional expression in the experience of personal identity (self feelings), whose origin and development we shall discuss in connection with the vicissitudes of object relations and identifications.

2

Review of Recent Literature on the Problem of Identity

THE PRECEDING discussion of the origins of self and object representations and of self awareness implies and demonstrates that I find myself in accord with the definitions offered by Greenacre (1958) and Mahler (1957), who have described the development of the sense or feeling of identity (self awareness, self feeling) in connection with the constitution of bodily and mental self images in the child. Eissler (1957), on the other hand, regards the self as an independent structure, comparable to the ego but developing only in adolescence. Thus he believes that experiences of identity arise likewise at that time. While I cannot agree with his hypotheses, the observations on which they are founded are certainly valid, as we shall see in the discussion of adolescence. Erikson (1956), although he speaks of identity formation as "a lifelong development" (p. 113), uses the term "ego identity" similarly to "denote certain comprehensive gains which the individual, at the end of adolescence, must have derived from all of his preadult experiences in order to be ready for the tasks of adulthood" (p. 101).

Under the influence of Erikson's papers, two books have recently been written on this topic: Wheelis's (1958) *The Quest for Identity* and Lynd's (1958) *On Shame and the Search*

[24]

for Identity. Like Erikson, these authors have a sociological orientation, but they carry it to quite an extreme. Whereas Erikson describes common identity disturbances in adolescence, they speak of the search for identity as a general problem of the whole present generation, a problem caused by the sociological changes of our time. Thus, loss or severe disturbances of identity are considered less from the individual and psychiatric than from the sociological point of view, in terms of generalized group phenomena. Lynd, who leans heavily on both Erikson's and Sullivan's work, simplifies matters considerably by stating that disturbances in the sense of identity arise when a person cannot "find aspects in his social situation with which he can clearly identify" (p. 215). Wheelis likewise describes mainly disturbances in the feeling of identity caused by the breakdown of the value systems of the past and by the resulting superego problems and confusions in the present generation.

Probably as a result of their sociological orientation, these authors, who both discuss the widespread or general occurrence of disturbances in identity formation and in the feeling of identity during and after adolescence, pay no attention to such problems in children or in psychotics, and ignore infantile development and the ontogenetic factors.

Originally Erikson did not overlook the genetic approach,[1] but he seems increasingly to remove himself from it. His studies on identity certainly place the focus mainly upon the adolescent and preadolescent period. This is reflected in his use of the terms ego identity and identity formation. Comparing his various definitions in "Ego Development and Historical Change" (1946) and in "The Problem of Ego Identity" (1956), I share his opinion that the term ego

[1] From the psychoanalytic point of view, I find his diagram of psychosocial crises (1956, p. 120) not too informative and somewhat misleading.

[25]

identity, as he employs it, "still retains some ambiguity." In the first-mentioned paper he equates it with "a more realistic self-esteem" which "grows to be a conviction that the ego is learning effective steps toward a tangible collective future, that it is developing into a defined ego within a social reality" (p. 23). Ego identity, defined as "the awareness of the fact that there is a selfsameness and continuity to the ego's synthesizing methods," is here (p. 23) explicitly distinguished from the feeling of "personal identity," inasmuch as it intends to convey not only "the mere fact of existence" but "the ego quality of this existence" (p. 23). No doubt the term ego identity in this sense lends itself readily to a psychosociological study which relates "individual identity" to "group identity." But I find it very difficult to distinguish personal identity from ego identity, all the more since Erikson links up the latter with "realistic self-esteem" and relates the individual superego to the value systems of the society in which the individual is reared.

Erikson seems to use the term ego identity very broadly, indeed much too broadly: he lets it "speak for itself in a number of connotations" (1956, p. 102) as referring to "a conscious sense of individual identity" or to "an unconscious striving for a continuity of personal character" or to "a criterion for the silent doings of ego synthesis" or to "a maintenance of an inner solidarity with a group's ideals and identity."

In her discussion of the development of the sense of identity, Greenacre (1958) also points out that it "is a term of flexible and functional rather than absolute meaning" (p. 613). She first describes very beautifully what we mean by the identity of an object, such as a house, and later on defines the sense of identity or awareness of identity as likewise involving "comparison and contrast with some emphasis on basic likenesses but with special attention called to obvious unlikenesses." Unfortunately Erikson does not distinguish sharply between these two perspectives: between the person's identity as it develops and can objectively be described, and the subjective experience of identity or the striving for it which reflects such objective identity formation. This ambiguity finds expression in the paragraph in which Erikson discusses the ego and the self (representations) and concludes that "Identity formation thus can be said to have a self-aspect and an ego aspect" (1956, p. 149; italics omitted).

I am inclined to regard Erikson's introduction of the term "identity formation"—referring to an objective process—as valuable, provided it does not apply merely to the ego and its synthetic forces. I would prefer to understand by identity formation a process that builds up the ability to preserve the whole psychic organization—despite its growing structuralization, differentiation, and complexity—as a highly individualized but coherent entity which has direction and continuity at any stage of human development. Normal identity formation undoubtedly depends on the effectiveness of the synthesizing, organizing functions of the ego; but I believe that processes of organization are operative in all structure formations of the psychic apparatus, including the superego. Moreover, normal identity formation appears to rest on the ability of the psychic organization to develop and achieve an optimal secondary autonomy of superego and ego in its handling of reality and of the drives, of intersystemic conflicts, and of tensions within all systems. The objective process of normal identity formation finds reflection at any stage of development in the normal subjective feeling of identity.

Inasmuch as the concept of identity formation puts the focus on an individual's self realization, the fulfillment of

his potentialities, and his role in society, it calls special attention to the relations of identity to the ego and superego
identifications and their final vicissitudes during and after
adolescence. Most of the authors on the subject point to the
close links between identity and identifications, but from
different angles. Mahler (1957) deals with this issue in describing disturbances or loss of the sense of identity in "as if"
types and in psychotic children. Greenacre (1958) states that
"Identity is closely related to identification, whether as an
inner process of psychic development or an act of recognition
by a human being toward an outer object, animate or inanimate" (p. 613). Spiegel (1959) concentrates on the "frame of
reference regarding internal states" and on the "pooling"
(p. 99) of isolated self representations, an issue definitely
related to the synthetic aspects of identity formation that are
stressed by Erikson. Spiegel describes disturbances in the self
feeling and the related reality feelings arising from rapid
changes of the ratio of single self representations to the whole
self as frame of reference, or from oscillations between narcissistic and object cathexis, or else from oscillations of this
very framework. In connection with this last point he refers
to the relations between self feelings and identifications,
without further discussion.

To return once more to Erikson: he believes that "The
final identity . . . is superordinated to any single identification with individuals of the past" (1956, p. 112) and that
"Identity formation . . . begins where the usefulness of
identification ends" (p. 113). This drastic statement deserves
thorough examination and clarification. It certainly shifts the
emphasis from the infantile stage to the adolescent and postadolescent period. Quite in contrast to Erikson, Lichtenstein
(1961), in a fascinating paper on identity and sexuality,
places the origin of identity formation back to the earliest

mother-child relationship. I must discuss at least some of the challenging ideas expressed in his comprehensive study.

Like Eissler and Erikson, Lichtenstein emphasizes the experiences of continuity in the normal feeling of identity. Thus his concept of identity "characterizes the capacity to remain the same in the midst of change," while the sense of identity is the "consciousness of such continuity of sameness" (p. 193). His definitions show that he shares my main criticisms of Erikson's ambiguous concept of ego identity, which fails to distinguish objective identity formation from the corresponding experience, and which, besides, restricts identity formation to the ego alone. However, Lichtenstein considers the concepts of identity and objective identity formation to be of unique significance for the understanding of human personality development. According to him, animals have a preformed adaptive identity, guaranteed by their inherited instinctive automatisms. Man, however, being both a biological and a historical being, has a historical existence, i.e., an existence with self-defined, self-created identity, for whose maintenance he must struggle forever. This is why Lichtenstein introduces the notion of an identity principle that controls all human development and has priority over any other principle or need, including the need for survival.

In my opinion, Lichtenstein's idea that man is "forever threatened with loss or breakdown of his identity" (p. 184) is not borne out by clinical observation. Were it valid, identity problems would certainly be predominant in all neurotics. This is not so. Serious identity problems appear to be limited to neurotics with specific narcissistic conflicts, and to borderline and psychotic patients.

Lichtenstein's conviction of the unique role of human struggle for identity is based on his objections, in principle, to our Cartesian way of thinking in terms of subject and

[29]

object. He believes in man's "fundamental symbiotic way of existing"—an idea related to Eissler's concepts. Hence, "man . . . must define his identity" and "defines himself as an instrument, an 'organ' serving a function" (p. 203). Lichtenstein consequently assumes that the essential function of nonprocreative human sexuality is the establishment of "the earliest and most basic outlines" of identity. He regards the symbiotic mother-child relationship as the beginning of human identity formation. I find this view acceptable, even though the child's separation from the mother and the resulting process of individuation seem at least as essential for human identity formation. Nor do I object to the statement that "The mother imprints upon the child not *an* identity, but an *'identity theme'* " (p. 208). But the pitfalls in Lichtenstein's thinking become obvious when he defines "a partnership of sensual involvement" as an interaction "where each partner experiences himself as uniquely and specifically capable of serving as the instrument of the other's sensory gratification" (p. 207). Such a concept logically leads to a denial of the role of aggression in man's relations to his *Umwelt* and in the process of identity formation. In consequence, contradictions must arise, which come to the fore in Lichtenstein's case presentation. At that point he is compelled to distinguish between normal and pathological symbiosis. In fact, I have found the need "to serve as the instrument of the partner's gratification"—or to use the partner for this purpose—only in preoedipally fixated, sadomasochistic patients who maintain fantasies of fusion with objects, such as Lichtenstein describes in his patient. His definition circumvents the selfish wish for gratification in normal sexual partnerships and the wish for individual self assertion in man's relation with his environment.

There is certainly a very valid core in Lichtenstein's reasoning. Human beings as well as animals are born with a potential capacity (*Anlage*) for mutually adaptive and mutually gratifying relations with their own species and with their *Umwelt* in general. To term this state of affairs "symbiotic" seems to me misleading; such a term excludes the struggle for survival, for which man and animal must be equipped. In fact, living organisms not only need, feed, and gratify each other; they may also fight each other to the point of extinction of the species. This double-faced interrelationship between living creatures and their *Umwelt* cannot be compared to the relationship of an organ to a whole organism or to the truly symbiotic mother-infant relationship, which normally do not involve a destructive struggle.

I have discussed Lichtenstein's ideas at some length because in the ensuing chapters I want to show what I have already indicated here; namely, how, beginning with the child's individuation, man's establishment of his identity and the corresponding identity feelings reflect the fact that at any stage he needs and acquires a double equipment. This double equipment enables him, on the one hand, to live with his *Umwelt* in a state of personal and social interrelationships, mutual adaptation, mutual gratification, and mutual need fulfillment; on the other hand, it enables him to assert himself—if necessary by fighting—in the service of his individual freedom and survival and that of his group or species within this *Umwelt*.

Moreover, human beings achieve full physical and mental maturity, ego and superego autonomy, instinctual and emotional mastery and freedom only after adolescence. Up to this time they learn to relate to their *Umwelt*, to function and assert themselves in it, through the medium and under the influence of their parents and other guides and teachers who convey to them the rules and standards of their society and

[31]

the reality of their *Umwelt*. To put it differently: the initial symbiosis between mother and infant partially continues throughout childhood in the child's interrelationship with his parents. It is a situation which yields only gradually to a position of autonomy and mutual independence, and which is during or after adolescence rather reluctantly relinquished by both parents and child![2] This and the slow biphasic sexual maturation of the human young account for the specific qualities of his interrelations and identifications with the parents, and for the outstanding but ultimately receding role of both in the gradual process of individuation.

I believe that only by virtue of tracing this process through all stages of childhood and adolescent development can we gain more definite criteria regarding the prerequisites for normal identity formation or the causes for pathology in this area, respectively. But it is already evident that identity formation must, at any phase, reflect man's complicated instinctual development, the slow maturation of his ego, his uneven superego formation, and the intricate vicissitudes of those object relations and identifications with his family and his social milieu upon which his individual personal, cultural, social adult life in and with his environment is founded.

---

[2] Frequently parents, especially mothers, develop depressive states when all their children have left the home.

3

The Fusions between Self and Object Images and the Earliest Types of Identifications

IN RECENT years, studies of the subtle interplay between mother and infant and of the harmful effect of early separation from or loss of the mother have called increasing attention to the psychology of motherhood and to the influence of maternal care on early infantile ego development. In view of our growing knowledge in this field and of the controversy aroused by Bowlby's papers (1958, 1960), I would like to begin my discussion of the precursors of object relations and identifications with some comments on our current concept of infantile orality.

Apparently, we must clearly spell out how far this concept must be, and practically has been, broadened over the years. We must emphasize that the infant's experiences during the primitive oral stage are certainly not limited to the feeding situation and to "oral" erotism in the narrow sense of this term. They extend to a broad variety of stimulating, gratifying, and frustrating experiences, to which the infant reacts with psychobiologically prepatterned (instinctive) responses, such as sucking, smiling, crying, clinging, and, later on, following, on which Bowlby lays such emphasis.[1]

For years, we have indeed been thoroughly familiar not only with the erotism of the mucous membranes and all areas of the skin (touch, temperature, and pain), but with the significant role of motor erotism, of acoustic and visual stimuli, and of proprioceptive and kinesthetic stimulating sensations in the child (Sadger, 1911; Fenichel, 1945). It is probable that most of these experiences originate in the earliest mother-child interrelationship. To be sure, we do not know precisely at what time the psychic apparatus becomes capable of retaining memory traces of pleasure-unpleasure experiences; but there is no doubt that long before the infant becomes aware of the mother as a person and of his own self, engrams are laid down of experiences which reflect his re-

---

[1] Schur (1960a), in an excellent discussion of Bowlby's erroneous conception of the child's instinctive reactions, relies on the psychoanalytic perspective as well as the viewpoint of modern ethology. Most of Bowlby's misunderstandings result from the fact that he erroneously regards the drive theory as a theory of "secondary drives." Confusing the terms "instinctive" and "instinctual" (1960), he inevitably ends up by giving up the psychoanalytic drive theory altogether. For reasons of clarification I may restate that "instinctive" behavior refers to innate, psychobiologically prepatterned motor and affectomotor responses which are in the service of individual survival and of the species, and which provide for the discharge of psychic ("instinctual") drive energy. Regulated by the pleasure-unpleasure principle, these responses are expressive of the "need to seek" and the "necessity to avoid." In other words, they serve partly the gratification of instinctual drives (hunger, libidinal and aggressive drives), and partly the avoidance of pain and the withdrawal from it. They develop in reaction to certain perceptions, such as those of instinctual needs and instinctual danger, of external stimuli and external danger. I may here refer to Schur's paper on "Phylogenesis and Ontogenesis of Affect- and Structure-Formation and the Phenomenon of Repetition Compulsion" (1960b, p. 284).

As a result of his conceptual and terminological confusion, Bowlby speaks merely of the infant's "physiological" and instinctive needs, but he does not even mention its libidinal instinctual needs, gratifications, and frustrations, and the corresponding pleasure-unpleasure experiences in which the child's emotional ties to the mother are rooted.

sponses to maternal care in the realm of his entire mental and body self.

As a matter of fact, in all probability the child's and his mother's drive-discharge patterns in general become tuned in to each other during the infant's first months of life. I believe that this is the meaning of Lichtenstein's statement that in the earliest symbiotic situation the mother imprints on the child an "identity theme." For this reason, disturbances of the psychophysiological equilibrium, resulting in anxiety, may be caused by separation of the infant not only from the breast but from the "whole mother," before the child can discriminate her from other persons.

This implies that awareness of object and self does not arise merely from strictly oral sources, but it does not confirm Bowlby's thesis of the insignificance of feeding and weaning experiences. Undoubtedly, hunger, oral libidinal tensions and their gratifications lead to unique pleasure-unpleasure experiences, which constitute the first and most significant bridge to the mother. And, as Schur underscored correctly, our clinical material furnishes ample evidence of the harmful effects of unfortunate weaning experiences. Moreover, Bowlby neglects the significant fact that the child's first visual impressions of the mother are connected with the feeding situation. It is the combined oral-visual experience of the breast—or primal cavity, respectively (Spitz, 1955)—that not only equates the mother with the breast but turns the latter into the first image of the gratifying mother. Subsequently, the memory traces left by any kind of libidinal stimulation and gratification in the past are apt to cluster around this primitive, first, visual mother (breast, primal cavity) image.[2] The same is true for the building up of self-images: the

[2] As Schur pointed out, the importance of the visual image was already emphasized in Freud's book on dreams (1900).

images of the orally gratified or deprived self will tend to absorb the engrams of all kinds of physical and emotional stimuli, satisfactions or deprivations experienced in any area of the whole self.

Thus, in a patient's associations, imagery and memory material referring to oral deprivations may express deprivations during infancy which were not merely oral in the narrow sense of the term but may have been experienced in the entire realm of the complex mother-infant interrelationship. Frequently, psychosomatic manifestations associated with such "oral" memory material give us special clues to the early infantile past.

The broadening of the concept of infantile orality is of special importance with regard to the influence of maternal care on the growth of the infantile ego.

The unique role of the close libidinal ties which develop between mother and infant is indeed epitomized by the multiplicity of their functions. The mothering attitudes and activities which provide the infant with libidinal stimulations, gratifications, and restrictions, and thus pave the way to his emotional attachments, concomitantly turn the mother into his external ego and secure his survival. But, in addition, these very same attitudes and activities directly stimulate and promote his physical growth and the mental growth of his ego and very soon begin to convey to the child the reality principle and the first moral codes.

Regarding the direct influence of maternal care on the child's physical and mental growth, his stimulus hunger and the role of pleasurable stimulation by the mother deserve special emphasis (Fenichel, 1945).

We know that the mouth and hands serve as the main instruments in the child's first endeavors to discover the object world and his own bodily self (Hoffer, 1949). But from the viewpoint of his general ego growth and the development of functional activity, stimulating motor, proprioceptive, kinesthetic, touch and temperature, acoustic and visual pleasure experiences may be of even greater significance.

In fact, when a mother turns the infant on his belly, takes him out of his crib, diapers him, sits him up in her arms and on her lap, rocks him, strokes him, kisses him, feeds him, smiles at him, talks and sings to him, she offers him not only all kinds of libidinal gratifications but simultaneously stimulates and prepares the child's sitting, standing, crawling, walking, talking, and so on, i.e., the development of functional ego activity. In my opinion, these considerations show convincingly that the mother's influence on the infantile growth of the ego cannot be conceptualized better than in terms of our drive theory.

So far, I have been mainly concerned with the introduction, clarification, and discussion of those concepts and conceptualizations on which my further investigations will rest.

But before we can turn to the formation of the ego, which proceeds under the influence of the energic and structural differentiation of the primal mental—or rather, psychophysiological—self, I must discuss the precursors of object relations and of the identifications which play such a paramount part in the child's ego formation and in the molding of individual personality traits.

Freud (1923) describes the establishment of ego and super-ego identifications in the chapter on "The Ego and the Super-Ego (Ego-Ideal)" in *The Ego and the Id*. His point of departure is the narcissistic identifications of the melancholic:

We succeeded in explaining the painful disorder of melancholia by supposing that, in those suffering from it, an object which was lost has been reinstated within the ego;

that is, that an object-cathexis has been replaced by an identification [see "Mourning and Melancholia," 1917b].

[He continues:] Since then we have come to understand that this kind of substitution has a great share in determining the form taken on by the ego and that it contributes materially towards building up what is called its 'character.'

At the very beginning, in the primitive oral phase of the individual's existence, object-cathexis and identification are hardly to be distinguished from each other. . . .

When it happens that a person has to give up a sexual object, there quite often ensues a modification in his ego which can only be described as a reinstatement of the object within the ego, as it occurs in melancholia; the exact nature of this substitution is as yet unknown to us. It may be that, by undertaking this introjection, which is a kind of regression to the mechanism of the oral phase, the ego makes it easier for an object to be given up or renders that process possible. It may even be that this identification is the sole condition under which the id can give up its objects. At any rate the process, especially in the early phases of development, is a very frequent one, and it points to the conclusion that the character of the ego is a precipitate of abandoned object-cathexes and that it contains a record of past object-choices. . . . We must also take into consideration the case of simultaneous object-cathexis and identification, *i.e.* in which the alteration in character occurs before the object has been given up. In such a case the alteration in character would be able to survive the object-relation and in a certain sense to conserve it [pp. 35-37].

In these remarks Freud outlines the problems on which we shall focus: the infantile development from primitive, so-called narcissistic, to meaningful ego and superego identifications and the differences between the former and the latter.

The earliest infantile stage is represented by the mother-child unit. Of course, this situation cannot yet be described in terms of identification, which is a process or the result of a process.

I have repeatedly stated that at first the infant can probably hardly discriminate between his own pleasurable sensations and the objects from which they are derived. Only when the perceptive functions have sufficiently matured can gratifications or frustrations become associated with the object. In the next chapter, I shall discuss more extensively the constructive influence of frustrating experiences on the discovery of and distinction between the self and the love object. Induced by such repeated unpleasurable experiences of frustration and separation from the love object, fantasies of (total) incorporation of the gratifying object begin to arise, expressive of wishes to re-establish the lost unit. This desire probably never ceases to play a part in our emotional life. Even normally, the experience of physical merging and of an "identity" of pleasure in the sexual act may harbor elements of happiness derived from the feeling of return to the lost, original union with the mother. The original intensity and survival of such wishes justifies Bowlby's stress on the significant role of separation anxiety, which appears about the sixth or seventh month.

These earliest wishful fantasies of merging and being one with the mother (breast) are certainly the foundation on which all object relations as well as all future types of identification are built.[3]

Let us view these fantasies more closely in connection with the child's instinctual activities at the age of about three months (Spitz, 1957, p. 119), when he is already able to

[3] I have deliberately avoided Freud's term "primary identification." It is somewhat ambiguous in so far as it appears to refer to the primary state of union with the mother, preceding discovery and cathexis of the object world, as well as to the preoedipal types of identification to be discussed below.

[39]

perceive the love object, or at least part objects, as different from himself. Whenever he is fed by his mother or is physically close to her body, his wishful fantasies of complete reunion with the mother by means of (oral and visual, respiratory, skin) incorporation will be gratified. Hence, with the achievement of gratification, his images of the self and of the love object will temporarily merge, only to be severed again with the increase of instinctual needs and experiences of hunger, frustration, and real separation, which are apt to arouse aggressive and libidinal desires.

Thus the hungry infant's longing for food, libidinal gratifications, and physical merging with the mother, which is the precursor of future object relations, is also the origin of the first, primitive type of identification, an identification achieved by refusion of self and object images. This refusion of self and object images will be accompanied by a temporary weakening of the perceptive functions and hence by a return from the level of beginning ego formation to an earlier, less differentiated state.

This type of identification plays a predominant role in the mental life of the baby throughout the preoedipal and early oedipal phase, and to some extent even later. In fact, it still finds its place within the mature psychic organization. I have referred above to the sexual experience in which the whole self seems to merge with the partner. I now wish to add that the adult ego will make extensive use of introjective and projective mechanisms, based on such fusions between self and object images, for the special purpose of establishing feeling and fantasy identifications at any level, not only with our love objects but with our whole environment. Our subtle, empathic understanding of others, especially those we love, depends on such temporary—either short-lived or more lasting—identifications. However, such *temporary* fusions induced in the service of the ego do not normally weaken the boundaries between the images of self and objects, whereas in the early infantile stage such firm boundaries have not yet been established. And as long as those fantasy and feeling identifications coexist and collaborate with mature personal relations and firmly established ego and superego identifications, they will not in any way affect a person's feelings of identity.[4]

Child analysts seem to agree that up to the age of three, conscious fantasies of merging with love objects are within the margin of normal development. But I have already stated that even far beyond the preoedipal period the unconscious self and object images tend rapidly to vary, separate, and merge again. Even when the child has progressed to a full awareness of himself and of his love objects as individual entities, his dependency on the mother for the satisfaction of most of his instinctual needs and the execution of his ego functions is still bound to prevent the complete separation of maternal and self images. Instinctual gratifications, physical and emotional closeness, the support, protection, and guidance offered by the mother, all tend to join them again and again; so that in general the maternal (and paternal) image will continue for some years to be only an extension of the child's image of his self, or vice versa. This is what lends the child's relationship to his mother such "narcissistic" qualities. His involvement in the mother is of dramatic intensity. But even when she is no longer exclusively a need-gratifying object but has become the object of touching

4 I may mention that individuals or groups who are under any sort of terror (catastrophies, authoritarian regimes) may quickly regress to magic experiences of merging either with each other or with the torturer or dictatorial leader. I believe that this mechanism partly accounts for the fatal group reactions in a panic, or for certain reactions of people believing and blindly following a leader; or making false confessions when cross-examined under torture.

affection, the baby, as yet unable to love in the sense of caring for others, is still mainly concerned with his own precious self. Even though he must and does adjust to the parental attitudes, he cannot understand and respect the parental needs, unless they serve his own or are in accordance with them.

Whereas the above-described fantasies of fusion with the love object are rooted in the child's symbiotic interrelationship with the mother, a more active type of primitive identification develops from his increasing efforts to imitate the love objects. In *The Psychoanalytic Theory of Neurosis*, Fenichel (1945, p. 31) described the close connections and interrelations between the still predominantly receptive infantile fantasies of this period and the imitations of the love objects which begin in the first year of life but already require the participation of the motor apparatus. Since these imitations originate in the close, empathic ties between mother and child, they probably emerge from what we may call primitive affective identifications. The fact that the mother is able directly to induce affects in the baby by way of her own affective expression—a fact on which Sullivan's anxiety theory is based—is well known, but difficult to explain. Observations on infants leave little doubt that the child very early begins to perceive, to respond to, and to imitate the gestures, the inflections of voice, and other visible and audible affective manifestations of the mother. I have already spoken of the mutual "tuning in" of the mother's and child's discharge patterns, and discussed how the mother's interplay with the infant stimulates and prepares his awakening emotional life and his ego functions. We may surmise that the child's imitation of parental emotional expression arises on this basis and that early reciprocal affecto-motor identifications between mother and child precede and

[42]

usher in the child's imitations of the parents' functional activities.

The child's expanding motor activities, his learning to walk and to talk and to behave like the parents, his cleanliness training, which is expressive of a beginning instinctual control—all these accomplishments certainly mark the progress of ego formation. But his playful imitations of what the parents do are at first only forerunners of true ego identifications, just as his beginning reaction formations are but the precursors of superego formation. In fact, we must not speak of ego identifications before the child begins to develop ego attitudes and character traits taken over from the parents, and before he manifests true ego interests and practices meaningful ego functions guided by their example and their demands.

In the beginning the baby's imitations of the mother, of her gestures, her behavior, her actions, are indeed only formal "as if" activities without awareness of their meaning, founded merely on the close links of empathy with the mother. It is not yet their essential goal to achieve a real likeness to the love objects. At this stage the child is still apt to believe that imitating the mother, "playing mother," means being or becoming the mother. Such magic, illusory fantasies indicate how much the child wants to maintain the mother as a part of himself and to adhere to the primitive aim of merging with her without distinction and consideration of the external and his own, inner reality.

The main progress manifests itself in the child's growing desire to achieve this goal no longer only through sensual gratifications and physical closeness with the love object but also by activity of his own. However, his insufficient capacity for perception of reality still permits him to join and to expand his images of objects and self in accordance with his wishful, magic fantasies, regardless of the love objects' and his own limitations.

This is the period of constant cathectic shifts and changes, to which I have already referred above. Libido and aggression are continuously turned from the love object to the self and vice versa, or also from one object to the other, while self and object images as well as images of different objects undergo temporary fusions and separate and join again. Simultaneously, there is a tendency to cathect one such composite image unit with libido only, while all the aggression is directed to another one, until ambivalence can be tolerated. These cathectic processes are reflected in introjective and projective mechanisms based on the child's unconscious fantasies of incorporation and ejection of the love object. At this stage the child displays submissive, clinging, following attitudes or behavior alternating with temporary grandiose ideas showing his "magic participation" in the parents' omnipotence. There are erratic vacillations between attitudes of passive, helpless dependency on the omnipotent mother and active, aggressive strivings for self expansion and a powerful control over the love objects.

In his interesting studies on elation, Lewin (1950) has traced the genetic origin of these opposing active-aggressive and passive-submissive attitudes to different phases in the child's earliest experiences of oral gratification. The desires either to make the mother part of himself or to become part of her appear, indeed, to be derived from fantasies of either devouring the love object or being devoured by it. According to Lewin, they go back to the two phases of oral gratification: the first, in which the child aggressively seizes and drinks from the breast; and the second, in which he relaxes, becomes passive, and finally (reaching the third phase) goes to sleep.

The increasingly contradictory, either passive-submissive

or active-aggressive behavior of the child during the preoedipal and early oedipal period goes hand in hand, of course,
with his ambivalent emotional fluctuations between loving
and trusting admiration of his omnipotent parents and disappointed, distrustful depreciation of his love objects. The
magic fantasy world of the preoedipal child is only gradually
relinquished; its remnants certainly survive the oedipal
period. We remember from our quotation above (Chapter 1)
that Freud (1914), in "On Narcissism: An Introduction,"
described the megalomanic attitudes of children, primitives,
and schizophrenics, their belief in the omnipotence of
thoughts and in the magic of words, as evidence of "primary
narcissism." Actually, however, these attitudes appear to be
manifestations of beginning "secondary narcissism" or, as we
should rather say, of preoedipal stages of ego formation and
of a beginning establishment and cathexis of self and object
images, with as yet weak boundaries between them. To these
stages the psychotic ego appears to regress.

We found on the other hand that Freud, though recogniz-
ing the "narcissistic identifications" of melancholics as
genetically earlier mechanisms, in *The Ego and the Id*
related them to the ego and superego identifications without
commenting on the characteristic and highly significant differences between these two mechanisms.

Observations of schizophrenic and manic-depressive psychotics, which are highly informative with regard to the early
stages of ego formation, indeed confirm the genetic connections between such primitive and the true ego and superego
identifications, but they also bring into relief their conspicuous differences.

Regarding the earliest types of identifications I repeat that,
magic as they are by nature, they are founded on primitive
mechanisms of introjection or projection corresponding to

fusions of self and object images which disregard the realistic differences between the self and the object. They will find expression in illusory fantasies of the child that he is part of the object or can become the object by pretending to be or behaving as if he were it. Temporary and reversible in small children, such ideas in psychotics may turn into fixated, delusional convictions. Regardless of reality the melancholic will indeed hate and accuse himself as though he were the love object, whereas the schizophrenic may even consciously be convinced that he is somebody else (Jacobson, 1954b).

I shall here interpolate some remarks on the mechanisms of introjection and projection, on which all forms of identifications are founded, with special reference to Melanie Klein's ideas on object image and superego formation.

Theoretical precision suffers quite generally from our failure to make clear distinctions between external objects and their endopsychic representations. But Melanie Klein (1934) compounded this confusion by failing to distinguish the latter from what she and her followers called "internalized" or "introjected" objects, or simply "introjects," and to define the meaning of these terms precisely. Her concepts are all the more misleading, since she equates the "introjects" with the infantile superego.

To begin with, the terms introjection and projection refer to psychic processes, as a result of which self images assume characteristics of object images and vice versa. The mechanisms of introjection and projection originate in early infantile incorporation and ejection fantasies and must be distinguished from them. They undergo elaborate vicissitudes, may be employed in the service of defense, and, in psychotics, are used for purposes of restitution.

During the preoedipal-narcissistic stage, gross primitive

[46]

introjective and projective mechanisms, in conjunction with pleasure-unpleasure and perceptive experiences, participate in the constitution of self and object images and, hence, of object relations. The small child's limited capacity to distinguish between the external and internal world, which is responsible for the weakness of the boundaries between self and object images and the drastic cathectic shifts between them, promotes the continuous operation of introjective and projective processes. Thus, it is quite true that during the first years of life the child's self and object images still have more or less introjective and projective qualities.

But the establishment of realistic object and self representations rests increasingly on the maturation of perceptive and self-perceptive functions, i.e., on reality testing, at the expense of projective and introjective mechanisms. However, while becoming more and more subtle and refined, the latter continue to play an essential part in the processes of identification and in the advance from primitive fusions to those selective identifications on which infantile ego and superego development rests.

Hence, in adult patients, we must not confuse transference processes based on displacement from one object image to another, such as from the mother onto the analyst, with projections. Naturally, projection mechanisms may be involved in transference phenomena, e.g., when the analyst becomes the representative of the patient's superego or also of his id strivings. It is equally incorrect to describe the object or self images of normal or neurotic adults simply as "introjects." Introjections of object images into self images or projections of self images onto object images are actually characteristic of psychotic identifications. Moreover, psychotic patients may develop delusional projective object images which they may never attach to definite, external persons. They may also develop delusional self images through introjection of early infantile object images which hardly resemble any past or present realistic external objects.

Melanie Klein's ideas on "internalized" or "incorporated" objects (1934, p. 287) appear to be inferences drawn from observations on very young children and on psychotic or borderline patients who show interesting intermediate stages in the constitution of realistic object and self representations. Such patients may at times experience their mental functions or their body organs as belonging to their own self and, at other times, as objects, i.e., as foreign bodies which they want to expel. Or they may at one time attach parts of their own mental or body self to external objects, and at another time attribute realistic object qualities to the latter. In small children, their "transitional objects," which Winnicott (1953) has so magnificently described, are a characteristic expression of such intermediate stages in the advance from narcissistic to true object relations.

Observations of this kind are certainly very instructive and helpful for detailed studies of the developmental period that I have been discussing. They also raise the question whether the establishment of object images might not represent a compromise solution between the small child's ambivalent tendencies to make the "good" love object part of his self and to eliminate the "bad" object from it. In so far as the object images are "endopsychic" formations, they certainly have become part of the inner world, i.e., of the self; but by being distinguished as objects from the image of the self, they become separated and kept apart from it.

In conclusion, I should emphasize that Melanie Klein's observations have proved to be very valuable. But her theoretical conclusions are untenable, and her terminology is extremely confusing.

[48]

4

The Child's Discovery of His Identity and His Advance to Object Relations and Selective Identifications

As THE CHILD enters his second year of life, changes in the nature of his relations to the object world set in, which are indicative of his gradual transition from the early infantile symbiotic phase to the stage of individuation and of beginning secondary ego autonomy. They mark the introduction into the psychic organization of a new time category, the concept of the future. Moreover, they presuppose the ability to distinguish single physical and mental features of the love objects, to compare and to perceive differences between objects—animate and inanimate—as well as between the objects and the self. When the child has advanced to this point, his narcissistic strivings begin to take a new turn: their aims change. Expressive of the child's rapid body growth and the growth of his ego, ambitious strivings develop which no longer revolve exclusively about wishes to control magically the love objects on which he depends. In their stead, ambitious efforts for realistic achievements can be observed, which seem in part to be independent of the child's instinctual needs. But under the influence of his instinctual conflicts these strivings soon become highly

[49]

charged with aggressive energy and find increasing expression in competitive struggles with admired, powerful love objects, in particular with his rivals. As these trends develop, the child's desires to remain part of his love objects, or to make them part of his own self, will slowly recede and give way to wishes for realistic likeness with them. This goal can be achieved by virtue of selective identifications, based on mechanisms of "partial introjection."

Evidently, this new and advanced type of identifications represents a compromise between the child's need to retain the symbiotic situation, to depend and lean on the need-gratifying, protective, and supportive love objects, and opposing tendencies to loosen the symbiotic ties by way of aggressive, narcissistic expansion and independent ego functioning. Under the influence of oedipal rivalry, this conflict will reach its first climax toward the end of the oedipal period and will then be resolved by superego formation. But it will be intensely revived during adolescence, and come to its final peak and find its definite solution in the adolescent's rupture of his oedipal ties and the establishment of ego and superego autonomy.

To return to the preoedipal child, it seems that his identifications with the mother, both as the aggressor (A. Freud, 1936, 1949) and as the person who imposes instinctual restrictions (A. Freud, 1936), pave the way to these new processes of identification. In contrast to his magic fantasies of fusion and his primitive affective identifications and merely formal imitations, they have a meaningful content and a realistic aim. Such an aim can be reached by way of deep-seated modifications of the ego, which now really assumes certain characteristics of the admired object.

This presupposes a new stage in the development of the self images: the distinction between realistic and wishful self

[50]

images. In fact, the ego cannot acquire a realistic likeness to the love object unless admired traits of this object become enduringly introjected into the child's wishful self images. These wishful self images thus become expressive of both: of the child's own ambitions, of his own strivings for narcissistic expansion and ego growth, and of admired characteristics of his love objects. In so far as the realistic self representations become a mirror of the ego, they now begin to reflect the traits actually taken over from the object of identification, so that a likeness between object and self images can now be experienced on a realistic basis. This new step in the development of the self images and the growing distinction between wishful and realistic images of the self are so meaningful because they are a prerequisite for the establishment of ego ideal and ego goals, i.e., of realistic goals regarding the future. This will be discussed below.

But I may here emphasize that the growing distinction between wishful self images and realistic self representations has very significant implications regarding the development of the feelings of identity.

Whereas the child's wishful self images increasingly give him direction by pointing to potential changes in the future, his representations of the actual self point to his present state and to the past stages in his development. Thus their differentiation must strengthen the feeling of selfsameness in spite of continuous changes.

Of course, the child will be protected from relapses into the world of magic fantasies of fusions and early infantile types of identifications to the extent to which he succeeds in building up true object relations which no longer display the narcissistic qualities described above. This again presupposes the constitution of well-defined self representations separated by distinct, firm boundaries from the likewise realistic representations of his love objects.

However, I cannot follow up the fascinating interplay between these developmental processes without first trying to derive some orientation from a preliminary schematic survey. Its sole purpose is to correlate the various stages of energic and structural differentiation to the constitution and cathexis of object and self representations, and to the corresponding ideational, affective, and functional development.

We may visualize the process of structural and energic differentiation as passing through the following infantile stages:

1. The primal (embryonal) condition of diffuse dispersion of undifferentiated drive energy in the unstructured "primal" psychophysiological self; discharge occurs predominantly by silent physiological processes.

2. With birth, growing cathexis of the perception and memory systems, of the motor apparatus and of the pregenital erogenous zones sets in; pleasurable and unpleasurable sensations begin to be perceived and become attached to, though still confused with, beginning outside perceptions. Energic differentiation occurs; libidinal and aggressive cathectic gathering poles are formed around nuclei of as yet unorganized and disconnected memory traces. Discharge to the outside begins by way of primitive, biologically prepatterned (instinctive) reactions to internal and external stimuli. Affective organ language develops.

3a. The stage of beginning structural differentiation and ego formation. Pleasure principle and "primary process" prevail. Unconscious (early preoedipal) fantasy life, pregenital sexual and affectomotor activity begin to develop, although affective organ language is still predominant. Multiple, rapidly changing and not yet clearly distinguished part images of love objects and body part images are formed and linked up with the memory traces of past pleasure-unpleasure experiences and become vested with libidinal and aggressive forces. Corresponding affect components arise; impulsive affectomotor reactions to external and internal stimuli change in quick sequence, reflecting the variability of unconscious imagery, the cathectic fluidity, and the tendency to immediate drive discharge; signal affects begin to become effective.

3b. When the child learns to walk and talk and acquires urinary and bowel control, a more organized stage sets in. Object and self awareness grows, perception and organization of memory traces expand. The object imagery gradually extends to the surrounding animate and inanimate world. Language symbols, functional motor activity, and reality testing develop. But magic animistic fantasy life, preverbal at first, predominates and remains concentrated on the mother until preoedipal and later oedipal triangle configurations shape up. Object constancy develops. Specific affect qualities and more sustained emotional states come into being, influenced by increasing formation of countercathexes.

4. Infantile sexuality reaches its climax; fusion and neutralization of sexual and aggressive drives has set in. Thought processes are organized, functional motor activity and object relations develop rapidly. Accordingly, single affects begin to merge into compound fusions. Emotional and instinctual control is being established; tension tolerance increases. Preponderance of libido and enduring libidinal object investments develop. As tender attachements grow and affects become attached to ego functions, awareness of self begins to extend to awareness of emotional and thought processes, of ego attitudes and ego functions. A concept of the self as an entity that has continuity and direction is formed. Reality principle and "secondary" process become more dominant.

[53]

Signal anxiety (castration fear) exerts a drastic influence on repression and countercathectic formations.

5. Drive neutralization is greatly enhanced by superego formation; the latency period begins. Physical and mental activities make rapid progress; conceptual thinking develops and expands; maturation and structural organization of ideational and emotional processes advance with the growing ability of the ego to bind down psychic energy in enduring cathexes; increasingly realistic preconscious representations of the animate and inanimate, concrete and abstract object world are formed, and can be stabilized by their firm and lasting cathexis with libidinal, aggressive, and neutralized forces. The superego establishes a lasting and dominant control over the cathexis of the self representations. Superego fear becomes the leading affect signal. In the process of final taming, repatterning, modification, and organization of the affects under the influence of the superego, enduring feelings and feeling states develop on a large scale as an expression of the ego's state and reactivity. The subtle differentiation of the emotional qualities proceeds hand in hand with an increasing awareness of the qualities of emotional experiences. These changes and the establishment of physical, intellectual, and moral achievement standards enhance the experience of a consistent self that maintains its continuity despite changes.

We know, of course, that the most influential factor in the child's development is the child-parent relationship, whose part in the building up of the ego we may summarize briefly as follows. Parental influences stimulate the growth of the ego and support the control, partial inhibition, partial fusion, neutralization and utilization of sexual and aggressive drives in the service of the ego and of "secondary"-process functioning. Thus they contribute greatly to the psychosexual

[54]

development and the maturation of feelings, thinking, acting, and the sense of reality, and promote the establishment of aim-inhibited personal and social relations and of solid identifications with the love objects in the ego and superego. In general, they promote the child's gradual individuation and his advance from the psychobiologically determined dependency situation to independent ego activity spreading out to social, cultural, and eventually ego-syntonic sexual pursuits.

Even though we are sufficiently familiar with the parental influence on infantile development, we must at least focus on certain aspects of it which are significant in the present context. To be sure, the goal of education as I outlined it above can be reached only in an atmosphere of parental love and care, with sufficient libidinal stimulation and gratification. Since it promotes the establishment of stable, enduring libidinal cathexes both of the objects and of the self, parental love is the best guarantee for the development of object and self constancy, of healthy social and love relations, and of lasting identifications, and hence for a normal ego and superego formation. However, the instinctual and emotional frustrations and prohibitions, combined with parental demands and stimulation of social and cultural pursuits, also make significant contributions to the development of an effective, independently functioning, and self-reliant ego.

They teach the child to relinquish not only his preoedipal and oedipal sexual drives but also his early infantile magic expectance of support, protection, and wish fulfillment from without. On his way to this goal, the child passes through experiences of continual deprivations, hurt, frustration, and disappointments in his parents, which arouse intense feelings of ambivalence. Although dangerous, the child's ambivalence conflicts can be utilized by the ego for very

[55]

constructive purposes. We remember that at first the child wants to take in what he likes and to spit out what he dislikes; to ascribe to his self what is pleasant and to the "strange" outside object what is unpleasant. In other words, he tends to turn aggression toward the frustrating objects and libido toward the self. Hence frustrations, demands, and restrictions, within normal bounds, reinforce in principle the process of discovery and distinction of objects and self; they throw the child back upon his resources and stimulate progressive forms of identification with the parents, which open the road to realistic independent achievements. Enhancing the narcissistic endowment of his ego, they promote the eventual establishment of secondary ego and superego autonomy.

Yet overgratifications, no less than severe frustrations, tend to induce regressive fantasies of reunion between self and love object. Constant overgratification or excessive frustration may therefore delay the child in establishing firm boundaries between the objects and the self, and hence may interfere with ego and superego formation and with the normal process of individuation. However, there are other and even more dangerous parental attitudes which may arrest this process. They are connected with the child's prolonged and only gradually receding symbiosis with his parents, which we must now examine more carefully from the viewpoint of the parents.

The earliest relationship between mother and child is of a truly symbiotic nature, for not only does the helpless infant need the mother and feed on her, but the mother also needs and—emotionally—even feeds on the child. This has been beautifully described by Benedek (1959), who showed how at any developmental stage the parents identify with their child's needs by reviving their own experiences of this phase. The significance of these mutual identifications between parents and child for the development of the sense of identity had been stressed by Greenacre (1958). But Benedek also emphasized that the childhood memories which the child revives in his parents not only induce identifications with him but also fortify the parents' identifications with their own parents (his grandparents). With regard to the child's individuation, it is indeed important to visualize the interplay between these double identifications in parental attitudes, and to consider their different roles and nature. The parents' identifications with their own parents have a long history. These identifications have modeled their ego and superego and remain the stronghold of the parental position, although different aspects are revived and brought to awareness by the child's changing stages. The parental identifications with the child are of a different order. Born of memories of the infantile past, they are limited to passing and changing fantasy and feeling identifications only, which serve the empathic understanding of the child and must be kept in bounds so as not to undermine the parental position.

In discussing the development of empathy, Olden (1953, 1958) has shown how a mother's empathic understanding of her child suffers when she actually steps down to his infantile level or, the reverse, when she expects the child to react or act on her own level. In either case the mother is unable to distinguish the child's need from her own and to subordinate her own identifications with the child to a loving acceptance of him as a separate individual. Even in the earliest symbiotic stage of the mother-infant relationship, the best emotional climate is indeed one in which the mother prepares the process of the child's individuation by a kind of maternal love that is aware of the differences between her own and the child's needs and roles, and tries to gratify both. In fact, parental attitudes betraying the tendency to sustain

[57]

a symbiosis with the child by "merging" with him are harmful in many respects. In recent years such pathological types of prolonged symbiosis between mother and child have been the subject of many studies, especially on psychotic children (Mahler and Elkisch, 1953; Mahler, 1957; Elkisch and Mahler, 1959).

Suffice it here to emphasize that such fantasies of merging with the child can be observed in cases where parents sacrifice their own needs to those of the child to the point of self extinction, as well as in situations where they either overprotect or dominate the child and keep him passive and dependent, or treat him as but an extension of their own self, ignoring his individual needs and sacrificing them to their own narcissistic requirements. All such attitudes increase the potential dangers to the preoedipal ego and to the superego precursors—dangers arising from the symbiotic nature of the mother-child relationship and from the indistinct line of demarcation between maternal and self images in the child. The child's fear of separation and his desire to maintain or regain the original mother-child unit are so strong, even normally, that he tends to resist the acceptance of sharply defined boundaries between his self and the mother.

It is pertinent in this context to emphasize once more that the small child's fantasies of fusion with his love objects are expressive of the early infantile situation, in which he must actually borrow the mother's ego for his own need fulfillments. If this situation is maintained for an unduly long period, the child's object relations may remain fixated forever at this primitive narcissistic level. This may be caused by unfavorable parental attitudes of a narcissistic, masochistic, or hostile, neglectful, overdepriving, or overgratifying and overprotective nature. But it may also be the result of a constitutional weakness, deficiency, or retarded maturation of the infantile ego, which may compel the child to lean heavily on the mother's ego for need gratification, support or control. The normal child seems to show the first signs of awareness of a "non-I" (Spitz, 1957) around the age of three months. Precisely how the development of self imagery and of self awareness proceeds from then on is a question which is difficult to answer, at least with regard to the first year of life. At any rate, to the extent to which the child begins to cathect and employ the executive organs of his own body and to acquire the physical and mental functions that will turn him into an autonomous, independent human being in his own right, he will be ready to develop the outlines of his future identity and, concomitantly, to build up advanced forms of personal interrelations and identifications.

In general, about the age of two or two and a half years the child's ego maturation, his ability to walk and to talk, the ever-widening scope of his perceptive and locomotor functions, his increasing manual accomplishments, his weaning and cleanliness training, etc., have advanced enough to bring about the startling discovery of his own identity, the experience of "I am I." It must be understood that this discovery does not imply that the child has already built up an enduring, consistent concept of his self as an entity. This concept undergoes many changes, and induces an increasing feeling of direction and continuity as the psychic organization grows, becomes differentiated, structured, organized and reorganized, until maturity is reached.

The child's discovery of his identity occurs in the wake of important changes in his relations to his first·love objects—changes which contribute a great deal to his individuation and his awakening sense of identity. From the observation of early infantile and psychotic imagery we may infer that in the child's first object images—apart from their projective features—perceptions of different objects probably become merged into varying image composites. But, significantly, the child, already at the age of about eight months, sometimes even earlier, begins to distinguish different objects: his mother from his father, from the nurse, from strangers, etc.[1] The distinction between objects can probably proceed more rapidly and consistently than the distinction between self and objects, because perception of the external world is easier than self perception and, besides, because the child normally has less instinctual motivation for a fusion between different objects than for a re-merging with his mother. In fact, the child's insatiable instinctual appetites stimulate his ability to discriminate between persons who may offer him supplementary gratifications and those who bar his way to need fulfillment. In any case, the beginning constitution of boundaries between images of different objects ushers in the development of specific and different relations to his various love objects. Concomitantly the child's first envy and rivalry conflicts take shape, conflicts which have a decisive influence on the processes under discussion.

At this point Greenacre's (1958) statement on identity, referring to likenesses with others and to differences from them, begins to become pertinent. Of course, experiences of likeness are bound to arise from the child's close intimacy with his mother and, as Greenacre stresses, will be favored by the mutual affective identifications between mother and child, to which I referred above. But what about the experiences of differences, which are a prerequisite for the development of identity feelings?

We know that by the end of the first year, the little boy or girl begins to show definite aquisitiveness, possessiveness,

[1] At about fifteen to eighteen months he starts using "no" (Spitz, 1957).

[60]

and manifestations of envy. To be sure, these ambivalent acquisitive wishes and the child's oral envy, which soon induce intense feelings of rivalry toward the father, siblings, and other objects, are the strongest incentive for his first comparisons. They teach him to distinguish, first, between his needs, his gratifications, and his frustrations; then between his and others' gratifications, and between his belongings and those of others. Passing through many frustrations, disappointments, failures, and corresponding hostile experiences of envy, rivalry and competition, the child eventually learns the difference between wishful and more or less realistic self and object images. Thus, not only the loving but also the hostile components of the infantile self- and object-directed strivings furnish the fuel that enables the child to develop his feeling of identity and the testing of external and inner reality, and on this basis to build up his identifications and object relations. This again calls attention to the significant role of aggression in these developmental processes, which has been stressed by Freud and other authors.

At first the child's acquisitive strivings are of course concentrated on his mother. But as soon as he discovers that he has rivals, he begins to displace the envious hostile impulses provoked by his frustrations from the mother onto these rivals. Projecting his own instinctual desires onto them, the child now wants to acquire what they possess and apparently received from the mother. From wanting the same gratifications and possessions as the rival, there is only a short but decisive step to looking for likeness and wanting likeness with him. Increasing love and admiration for the superior and also gratifying rival will reinforce this quest. However, frustration, hostility, and envy will compel the child also to take cognizance of such differences as may be responsible for his frustrations and shortcomings.

[61]

We noted above that the child's need to keep the "good," gratifying love object as part of himself, and to spit out and rid himself of the "bad," frustrating object, tends to throw him on his own resources, to increase the narcissistic endowment of his ego, and to stimulate ambitious strivings for narcissistic expansion and independent accomplishments. Now we may add that his feelings of envy and rivalry, while arousing desires for likeness, will propel him more forcefully toward delineations from his rivals than toward distinction from his main love object, the mother. Moreover, these feelings will promote his discrimination between such rival objects.

The mother-infant relationship must certainly be regarded as the matrix of identity formation, but the child's individuation which depends so greatly on separation from the object and on the discovery of differences soon gains momentum from his more ambivalent relations to his rivals than from his close intimacy with his mother.[2] Of course this simplifies matters considerably, since the child displays envy and rivalry feelings toward the mother as well, to the extent to which he develops closeness with his father and other rivals.

So far I have described how the child's finding of his identity, although dependent on the maturational growth of his ego, gains tremendous support from his beginning emotional relations to his first love objects and especially from his preoedipal envy and rivalry conflicts. I shall now focus on the influence which the child's identity feelings exercise upon his object relations and identifications. We realize that the discovery of his identity, which is so greatly promoted by aggressive forces, is a prerequisite for his gradual transition

2 I believe this is confirmed by observations of children in their second year. At that time they are already quite capable of perceiving that people differ from them, particularly if these persons arouse their envy and rivalry.

from the stage of primitive fusions and identifications with his love objects to the level of true object relations and of only partial and selective identifications with them. In fact, the child cannot establish emotional investments in other persons as objects which are different from his own self until he is able to experience his own identity; and since active strivings to acquire likenesses to others are also motivated by the discovery of differences from them, these strivings cannot develop either until the child has become aware of such differences.

Considering the infantile cathectic conditions, we realize, moreover, that enduring selective identification processes, which follow a steady course and direction and alter the structure of the ego consistently, cannot set in before the child's object-libidinal and narcissistic strivings have advanced to a certain level. The initially continuous vacillations between self- and object-directed cathexes and between the different object cathexes must have sufficiently subsided to permit comparatively lasting emotional investments in both: in objects and in the self. Such stable investments can only develop in the wake of processes of unification and consolidation of the object and self images. These processes call on the libidinal resources of the child, which are the indispensable ferment needed to forge "total" concepts from the opposing images of good and bad love objects and of a good and bad self.

I mentioned above the child's inclination to displace hostility from the mother to his rivals. Facilitating the gradual fusion of good and bad maternal images into a unified "good" but also sometimes "bad" mother, these shifts certainly assist the development of tension tolerance and of those feelings of pleasurable anticipation which introduce the category of time and secure the establishment of lasting emotional relations with the mother, i.e., of object constancy. This implies

[63]

that the development of personal relations with the mother precedes the acceptance of rival figures as total ("good" and also "bad") persons. This second step is not an easy achievement for the child. It must wait until his intense ambivalence toward the rival gradually subsides under the influence of reactive libidinal strivings, and his love wins out over the hostile, envious, jealous, derogatory feelings. The increasing prevalence of libidinal over aggressive investments concomitantly builds up the libidinal endowment of the self images, which is a precondition for the achievement of normal self esteem and for the formation of a unified concept of the self. Since the latter represents a decisive step in the development of identity feelings, this again underscores the all-important role of the libidinal forces in this process, and hence of the mother's love which helps to generate them.

I have emphasized the child's earlier delineation from the hated rivals, which soon promotes the development of his sense of identity more than does his closeness to the mother. Considering the identifications, in contrast to the object relations, it appears that this factor also tends more easily to induce partial identifications with rivals than with the main love object. To be sure, from an early age on, one can also observe identifications which appear to be induced primarily and predominantly by libidinal wishes to maintain, if not union, at least the utmost closeness with the love object, by virtue of actually becoming like it. Such identifications seem to arise directly from the child's earliest fantasy and feeling identifications with the mother rather than from instinctual conflicts. For this reason they hardly bear the imprint of the child's sexual and ambivalence struggles and do not become an important tool for his defenses. Predominantly centered about the main love object, such identifications can still be observed in adults, in situations of close intimacy, such as,

[64]

e.g., between marital partners who may ultimately resemble each other physically, emotionally, ideationally, and in their behavior.

In general, though, the infantile identification processes become increasingly centered about rival figures. This will be discussed more thoroughly in connection with the processes of idealization. At this point I should like to comment on Freud's assumption that identifications, being regressive in nature, tend to liberate aggression. Hartmann and Loewenstein (1962) regard this hypothesis as valid, as far as it refers to superego formation. I do not share their or Freud's opinion, which I believe is the result of inferences drawn from Freud's study of the narcissistic identifications in melancholics. I believe that it is the severe hostility of the psychotic toward his love object which, leading to inner object loss, makes him resort to regressive, primitive, narcissistic identifications, i.e., to fantasies of partial or total fusions with objects. But the selective ego and superego identifications of the normal child cannot be regarded as regressive phenomena of this type, since they do not arise in place of object relations. In fact, the child's object relations and identifications evolve hand in hand and exercise a mutually beneficial influence on each other. As I have emphasized, identifications seem actually to serve the absorption and neutralization of aggression, which can be vested increasingly in countercathectic formations and be discharged in ego functions. Regarding the beneficial influence of object relations on identifications, the latter are all the more successful, the more the child's libidinal forces predominate, and his ego, gaining strength, becomes able to tolerate frustration and to build up sublimations. For this reason, the preoedipal precursors of the superego still reflect, in part, the small child's own boundless cruelty, which cannot be toned down with the support of identifications. For the same reasons, enduring selective identifications with the predominant rival, the father, cannot be established before the child's loving feelings toward him are sufficiently strengthened to permit relations with him, too, as with a total "good and bad" person. In fact, the better the totality of other persons and of the self can be experienced, the more easily can the distinction, the perception of the differences between one's own self and others be tolerated, and likeness not only discovered but accepted, desired, and acquired.

This implies that the establishment of object and self constancy must be regarded as a very important prerequisite for both a healthy process of identification and normal superego formation. Conversely, the development of moral standards supports this merging of "good" and "bad" object and self images into concepts of total "good and also bad" persons and a total "good and also bad" self.

While this re-emphasizes the role of love in the establishment of sound identifications, they will forever reflect the inherent ambivalence to which they owe their existence. Indeed, any kind of identification implies: "I don't need you; if you don't want to do it for me, I can do it myself; and if you don't want to give it to me, I can give it to myself." While identifications thus display the child's touching dependency on his parents, they bring him closer step by step to the state of independence and to the time when the parents will become dispensable. Moreover, the selectivity of identifications increasingly expresses the child's rebellious struggle for the development and maintenance of his own independent identity, since it means: "In this respect I like you and want to be like you, but in other respects I don't like you and don't want to be like you; I want to be different, in fact myself."

[66]

The process of consolidation of self and object representations advances hand in hand with processes of increasing drive fusion and drive neutralization under the influence of ego formation. Just as discrimination between external objects precedes the distinction between them and one's own self, the experience of other persons' totality develops earlier than the concept of a unified self. In fact, the formation of such a concept depends not only on the child's libidinal investment in himself but on the general growth of the ego that leads to organization and coordination, correlation and interaction of sensory, instinctual, emotional experiences with ideational processes and with the perceptive and executive functions.

In this connection it is of interest that children with precocious ego formation seem to establish their identity at a very early stage and to show early signs of discriminating object relations. Displaying pride in their difference from others, they may even succeed very early in reversing roles with older siblings, not only by perceiving and aggressively exploiting their own advantages, but also by actually greater accomplishments.[3]

Of course, the interplay and interdependence of these

[3] I recently observed a precocious and rather aggressive little boy of one, who is already able to outdo his three-year-old brother by playing off his "role" as "the preferred baby." Whenever he covets the other's toys or food, he tries to snatch them away from the older child, crying righteously, "baby, baby!" His mother correctly interprets this as meaning: "*I* should get it; after all, *I* am the baby." At the same time this little boy begins to identify and compete actively, and sometimes successfully, with his more passive older brother. I would regard this behavior as evidence of the awakening feeling of his identity and of his particular role in the family group. He indeed acts, and already is regarded and treated, as the aggressive but uniquely advanced and adorable baby. His mutual interrelations with mother and grandmother appear to be affectionate but are already rather different in nature. The father and his interrelationship with his boys could not be observed.

developmental processes make it difficult to decide how far the precocious ego maturation of such a child is responsible for the early onset of his discriminating object relations, his identifications, his identity formation, or the reverse: how far his speedy object-libidinal development may influence and promote his ego formation. This was already implied in what I have said about the processes of identification. They begin to show direction and to become more enduring, more consistent and more selective, to the extent to which libidinal development makes progress and personal relations become stable and specified. This will be discussed in greater detail in connection with the child's finding of his sexual identity and his oedipal development. Here I want to stress the following point: only by becoming enduring, selective, and consistent, can identifications gradually be integrated, become part of the ego, permanently modify its structure, and support the organization and stabilization of the ego's defense system. This advances ego formation and the establishment of secondary ego autonomy and concomitantly the process of identity formation to the point where the child becomes aware of having a coherent self that has continuity and remains the same despite and in the midst of changes. Here the different influence on the feeling of identity of such enduring identifications with objects, as compared to primitive fantasy and feeling identifications, becomes apparent. Only the identifications which originate in enduring emotional object investments, and which result in gradual, consistent structural changes showing a definite direction, can fortify the inner feeling of continuity of the self. It is the proper balance between libido and aggression on which the success or failure of these processes depends. In case of a collapse of object relations because of oversevere hostility conflicts, such as can be observed in psychotic patients, we find indeed that their identifications break down simultaneously. Both may eventually be replaced by fusions with objects, which, involving fantasies of destroying them or being destroyed by them, may lead to experiences of *Weltuntergang* and loss of identity. We find in such patients fears of accepting and acquiring likenesses to others, in conjunction with an inability to perceive and tolerate differences from them, and to relate to them as to separate and different individuals. Likeness and difference are equally frightening, because likeness threatens to destroy the self and difference the object.

The role of libido as against that of aggression in such regressive fusions between self and objects becomes evident from a comparison between experiences of ecstasy in normal persons and fusion experiences in psychotics. Since normal experiences of ecstasy do not aim at destruction but are founded on a fantasy of libidinal union between self and object world, they result in a transitory sense of self expansion and the feeling that the self and the world are rich. Such experiences of merging, which may briefly retransform the images of the self and the object world into a fantasy unit vested with libidinal forces, permit an immediate re-establishment of the boundaries between them. By contrast, pathological regressive fusions caused by severe aggression may result in an irreparable breakdown of these boundaries and hence of the self and object representations.

5

The Child's Finding of His Sexual Identity and the Building Up of His Ego

In THE BEGINNING oedipal phase, the child's identity formation gains a strong impetus from his increasing genital interest, which centers the self- and object-directed cathexes about images of others' and his own genital organ. These preoccupations lead to the discovery of his sexual identity, a most significant component of personal identity. Greenacre (1958), concentrating chiefly on the contribution which the development of body images makes to the sense of identity, has described how this development is guided by oral-visual-manual investigations, particularly of the external body surface. She underlined "the continual reinforcement of the sense of the own self by the 'taking in' of a similar person" (p. 618), even at a mature age.[1] Greenacre furthermore discussed the significance of the facial and genital areas in "comparing and contrasting and establishing individual recognition of the body self." She emphasized the fact that the comparative invisibility of these areas—especially of the female genital—promotes fusions between the genital images of others and one's own. In this connection, I again refer to the inhibiting influence of the oedipal and castration conflicts

[1] I touched upon the same point in discussing experiences of depersonalization in persons thrown into an unfamiliar, strange environment (Jacobson, 1959).

on the constitution of realistic genital images. These conflicts result in the ubiquitous survival of castration fantasies in male and female adults, which resist the acceptance of the female genital as an undamaged organ. Moreover, the prohibition of manual genital play, i.e., of "touching," is certainly responsible for the child's usual overcathexis of visual perception, particularly with regard to seeing the genitals of others as well as his own. As a further result of this prohibition, the sexual interest is displaced from the "ugly" genital to the "pretty" body, and especially to facial appearance. In women this commonly leads to an intense narcissistic investment in their faces and figures. But we likewise observe in boys' attitudes toward girls a shift of interest from the "castrated" genital to the pretty facial and body appearance, an interest which may assume exaggerated forms. In some male patients, who as little boys used the opportunity to touch and stimulate little girls' genitals, the fear of manually exploring—and thereby harming—the "invisible" parts led to intense concentration on the girls' excited "visible," especially facial, responses. This served the denial of female castration by sustaining the firm conviction that little girls must and do have an invisible penis. To be sure, the little boy establishes his phallic position and hence his sexual identity more easily and readily than the little girl, who needs more time to form a realistic image of her genital, to accept it, and hence her feminine identity.

Greenacre has described the different—less visible—types of disturbances in the sense of identity in women caused by the invisibility of their genitals. But in view of the little girl's complicated sexual development and especially of her castration conflict, the question arises why, in general, women do not develop more severe and more frequent identity problems than men. Looking for an explanation, we must

[71]

realize that the child's experience of sexual identity does not by any means rest exclusively on genital comparisons. Since the strongest incentive for the development of perceptive functions is the child's instinctual and emotional strivings, his sexual curiosity is not limited to his own and others' genital organs but extends to his own and other persons' sexual activities. The child's primal-scene fantasies reflect his broad concern with his and others' psychosexual experiences. Moreover, as was shown above, the taboos and castration fears tend to shift his exploration and comparisons to other body areas. This is supported by the emphasis laid by adults upon general physical and mental male and female characteristics, rather than on the anatomical and particularly the genital difference between boys and girls. Under these influences, the experience of one's own and others' sexual identity soon expands to the whole bodily and mental person. Hence we can observe that little girls may establish their feminine identity long before they have settled their castration problems, or even if they never fully succeed in resolving them.

But this still does not sufficiently explain why women with "phallic" attitudes or "maternal" men, and even certain types of manifest male or female homosexuals, do not always develop very conspicuous disturbances in their feelings of personal identity. In some male and female homosexuals of this type, I found that their sexual and ego development had been determined mainly by identifications with a loving but dominant, active "phallic" mother. Even though their identification with this fictitious maternal image had led to manifest homosexuality, it had permitted their egos to develop sufficient stability, functional ability, and secondary autonomy to accept and eventually to integrate their sexual deviation well enough to build up a comparatively consistent and coherent concept of their self. Similarly, heterosexual women and men who unconsciously continue to adhere to the idea of an illusory female penis can sometimes integrate their "desirable" masculine (or feminine) traits rather successfully into the concept of their personal identity when these features are derived from identification with an acceptable "phallic mother."

Here I would even stress that the intermediary images of an invisible inner penis may potentially play a constructive role in the little girl's development. They may prepare her for a normal formation and acceptance of a realistic genital image (the vagina) and, in this case, pave the way to future genital responsiveness and the establishment of a feminine identity and position in adulthood.

Quite by contrast, I was able to observe profound identity problems in patients with latent or manifest homosexual conflicts, whose "feminine" attitudes and fantasies of having a "castrated genital" rested on severely masochistic identifications with a mother who played the part of the victimized, suffering, "castrated" woman. In such patients, the struggle against these identifications had seriously interfered with their ego development and identity formation. This shows that identity formation and the feelings of personal identity are not quite as dependent upon the heterosexual position as one might imagine: they are largely influenced by the extent to which consistent and enduring identifications leading to secondary autonomy and independence of the ego can be established, even if they lead to sexual pathology.

However, the eminent significance of the discovery of sexual identity by the child is self-evident. Considering the interrelations between this step and the vicissitudes of object relations and identifications during the oedipal period, let us remember that the preoedipal child's finding of his identity is a prerequisite for the onset of both true object relations and partial identifications with his parents. With the establishment of his sexual identity, a new influential factor arises. The preoedipal child, vacillating between heterosexual and homosexual, between active and passive strivings, still enjoys the freedom to assume, playfully, various roles: in fantasy, in attitudes or actions, on a more or less primitive ego level, he may alternately identify at one time with the father, at another with the mother, with an older sibling, or with a rival baby. I have also remarked that fantasies of merging with the mother are considered a normal phenomenon up to the age of three; but the child's discovery and establishment of his sexual identity, which reflect his instinctual advancement to the genital level, considerably reduce this freedom to play various roles.

Discovery and acceptance of the sexual differences assists both the boy's and the girl's gradual renunciation of desires to remain part of the mother and, hence, to remain "a baby." We know that the sexual vicissitudes of the little girl are complicated, since her oedipal relationship to the father is founded on her rejection of the female genital. But finally the mother will become the main model, and the sexual identification with her will help the little girl eventually to accept the female anatomy.

I believe that normally the little girl's reluctant acceptance of her feminine role may receive strong support not only from her father's seductive attitudes but also—strangely enough—from the derogatory attitudes she encounters in little boys. They "put her in her place" and thereby definitely show her, as it were, where she belongs: to the female sex. At this stage, friendships between girls and boys may be suddenly disrupted because the little boy, afraid of being thought a "sissy" if he likes to play with girls, turns away from them. His castration fears increasingly forbid him to seek their company, and arouse ardent desires to become part of a male group. At this stage even his practical dependency on his mother, strong as it is, tends to be more and more denied. His growing self assertion as a superior male toward the other sex, combined with his heterosexual strivings, promote phallic-masculine attitudes to the mother and other females. The recognition of anatomical likeness to his father, oedipal jealousy, competition, and concomitant admiration now definitely center his identification around the father.

As heterosexual drive impulses and aims take the lead, the wishful oedipal fantasies thus induce—in the boy earlier than in the girl—increasingly consistent and predominant identifications with the oedipal rival, while those with the love object of the opposite sex assume a subordinate role in the degree to which the latter becomes the definitely preferred love object. Thus the oedipal sexual and competitive strivings and the discovery of sexual identity not only stimulate the development of the child's object relations and identifications in general but also decisively influence their direction.

Subsequently there develops an increasing differentiation and hierarchic organization of the child's personal relations, ego interests, and identifications with objects of both sexes and different ages—processes which are terminated only in the course of adolescence. As we shall see in the next chapter, such processes of organization on the one hand play a large part in superego formation, and on the other hand gain enormous reinforcement from it.

Let us now consider the cathectic redistributions caused by the oedipal taboos and study, in particular, the interrelations between the advancing establishment of self and object representations and the development of ego interests and sublimations.

Toward the end of the oedipal phase, the influence of sexual prohibitions and castration fear reinforce affectionate attachments and drive neutralization in general. As the physical, ideational, and emotional development progresses, the images of all the executive organs will be increasingly cathected with more or less neutralized libidinal and aggressive forces at the expense of the genital and the pregenital erogenous zones. Desexualized thought and feeling processes gradually win out over sexual fantasies and impulses. Hand in hand with the gradual maturation of autonomous ego functions, the building up of ego identifications and object relations, of self and object representations advance further.

At that time, we observe highly significant and complicated energic transformations and cathectic changes, which greatly stimulate the development of sublimations and, more generally, of autonomous ego activity.

In *The Ego and the Id,* Freud (1923) describes the development of sublimations as follows:

> The transformation of object-libido into narcissistic libido which thus takes place obviously implies an abandonment of sexual aims, a process of desexualization; it is consequently a kind of sublimation. Indeed, the question arises, and deserves careful consideration, whether this is not always the path taken in sublimation, whether all sublimation does not take place through the agency of the ego, which begins by changing sexual object-libido into narcissistic libido and then, perhaps, goes on to give it another aim [pp. 37-38].

I believe that Freud refers in this paragraph to two different, though closely connected and interrelated processes. The pursuit of independent ego activities and sublimations

[76]

on the basis of ego and superego identifications with the love objects appears to involve the following cathectic shifts and changes: part of the libido vested in the love objects, after undergoing partial neutralization, is turned to other objects, especially in the area of ego interests. This promotes the constitution of new, animate and inanimate, object representations and of corresponding ideational and emotional processes and ego activities. Simultaneously, with the transition from the infantile dependence of the ego on the love objects to independent ego activity, in identification with them, libido is veered away from these object images to the self images. Thus, part of the object libido is transformed into narcissistic, self-directed libido which, joining forces with the libido withdrawn from the erogenous zones, is now used for the expanding cathexis of the executive organs and the functions of the ego, and consequently for the further building up of the self representations.

But we should again remember that the cathexes of the self representations, though deriving such powerful contributions from object-libidinal sources, are certainly founded on the original stock of psychic energy with which the whole mental self, including the images of the body and its functions that are the kernels of the future system ego, had been primarily vested. This assumption is reinforced by observations on schizophrenic children, such as those published by Mahler (1952, 1958). The autistic schizophrenic, the Kanner type, which she describes, appears to avoid any outside stimuli that would lead to contact with the object world. Unable to cathect objects, this type evidently develops primitive, defective self images which are primarily hypercathected at the expense of the object world. This certainly suggests that even in normal development the cathectic core of the self

[77]

images is the psychic energy originally vested in the primary psychophysiological self.

Moreover, not only do the self representations profit from the transformation of object libido into narcissistic libido, but the object representations in turn gain strength from reverse processes. Particularly during the early developmental stages, libido is continuously called away from the love objects and invested in the self, and again sent out from the self to the love objects (or their images, respectively). I shall come back to a consideration of these cathectic fluctuations when discussing the development of superego identifications.

So far I have neglected to consider the vicissitudes of aggression in the development of ego interests. In fact, the above-mentioned energic shifts and changes, although they are reinforced by the ambivalence conflict with the love objects, also facilitate its solution. The development of ego interests[2] calls away from the love objects not only part of the libido but also part of the aggression which, after being fused with libido and likewise more or less neutralized, can become vested in new personal and inanimate objects. At the same time the experience of learning how to function independently turns aggressive forces inevitably and increasingly away from the love objects toward the self, since the child in his beginning independent activities meets with constant hurts and failures. What he once experienced as disappointments and frustrations, hurts for which he blamed the parents alone, he now begins to regard partly as injuries that he has inflicted upon himself. This attitude is greatly supported by his efforts to master his aggression and to build up enduring

[2] It is useful to follow Mr. Kanzer's (1962) suggestion to distinguish ego interests, by which we mean object-directed pursuits, from self interest. The term self interest would refer to predominantly self-centered, egotistic-narcissistic strivings and pursuits of the ego.

libidinal relations to his love objects. Thus he is apt to undergo experiences of realistic physical and mental hurt, accompanied by feelings of "inferiority" and self criticism. They clearly manifest an increasing cathexis of the self representations with aggression turned away from the love-object representations. They indicate the onset of enduring self-directed aggression and potentially of a "secondary masochism," which in pathological cases may invade the psychosexual life, may color many ego attitudes and functions, or may develop mainly in the direction of moral masochism.

The latter is expressive of the profound and decisive influence that the internalization of parental demands and criticisms, beginning with the establishment of reaction formations and culminating in the constitution of the superego, exercises on the cathexis of the self representations with libidinal as well as with aggressive forces. This will be discussed extensively below.

But there is one step in this development on which I must focus in the present context. Speaking of the child's competitive comparisons with his rivals, I pointed out that they promote his testing of external objects and of his own self, and hence teach him to distinguish the omnipotent fantasies about his love objects and himself from the real objects and his real (potential and actual) self. As we shall see, a full realization of these differences will not set in before maturity and in some cases may never be attained. The role of this distinction in the constitution of ego and superego identifications will be discussed later on. Here I must underscore the point that a normal pursuit of ego interests presupposes sufficient awareness of the differences between grandiose narcissistic strivings and corresponding wishful self images on the one hand, and realistic ego goals based upon sound notions of the own self's potentials, i.e., one's own abilities, on the other.

The capacity for such a distinction develops under the influence both of failures and successes, of narcissistic hurt and expansion, of criticism and self criticism as well as of encouragement, approval and self approval, that is to say, of both libido and aggression.

My inquiry into the process of sublimation has aimed at describing the relations between ego activity and the corresponding cathectic processes involving the self and object representations. I may interject that for the purpose of establishing precise metapsychological conceptions it is advisable to distinguish more carefully than we commonly do, not only between the real objects and self and their respective mental representations, but also between ego attitudes and actions in the outside world and changes in the cathexes of object and self representations.[3]

From the foregoing discussion we must first of all conclude that we are not entitled to define (successful) ego activities simply as narcissistic gratifications. Even if they do not pertain to personal objects, their essential and central purpose is normally the pursuit of object-libidinal gratifications.[4]

---

[3] Already in 1942 Sterba pointed to the difference between the cathectic processes and the behavior in the realistic object world, and spoke of "the representation of the individual personality, that is the ego" (p. 61).

[4] At this point I wish to refer to Ernest Kris's writings and to some additional personal remarks by him on the subject of sublimations. Kris (1952) beautifully described the ability of creative persons to let their ego immerge into the id and emerge again, and thus, by oscillating between closeness to the id and distance from it, to use the id in the service of the ego. In further comments on this problem, Kris expressed his assumption that the capacity for sublimation was connected with a particular ability of creative people to draw and absorb psychic energy through manifold avenues from the deepest energic flux of the id, and to direct it into the channel of creative activity. This ability, I believe, presupposes a particular energic fluidity and elasticity in such persons, permitting rapid processes of drive transformation, drive fusion, and drive neutralization. This drive elasticity would account for

Let me describe what I mean with the aid of a practical example of a creative ego function, such as the writing of a book. First of all, the intention normally arises from a previous interest in and concern with the issue about which the author wishes to write. This issue is the object which must become enduringly vested first with libidinal, aggressive, and neutralized psychic energy to the point where the plan to write about it turns into action. Of course, the writing will never proceed if the writer does not have sufficient self assurance at his disposal, self assurance which must be based on an awareness and realistic evaluation of his abilities, and on a sufficient and sound cathexis of the function of writing. Even though his ego ideal and ambitious fantasies in general may be a further effective stimulus, his work will not be successful either if the main incentive for his writing is grandiose fantasies which surpass his abilities. As the author begins to write, he may "fall in love" with his book. Since

---

the capacity for such continuous fluctuations between id closeness and id distance during the creative process.

I would, furthermore, surmise that such an energic elasticity in creative persons may combine with a particularly favorable vicissitude of their orality, which enables them to hypocathect temporarily all other objects to an amazing degree and to hypercathect the one subject on which they work consistently with great amounts of energy, in a way remindful of the small child's exclusive oral investment in his single love object. But after achievement of their goal, such creative persons appear to be able to re-establish their previous cathectic balance until another creative spell ensues. I believe that this astounding ability becomes manifest in their "devouring" interest in their work, which during such creative spells makes them utterly forgetful of the rest of the world, and in their return to the common ways of life after its completion and relief from the tremendous creative tension.

Observations on the creativity of adolescents, to which I shall return in Chapter 11, suggest that this elasticity and fluidity in creative persons may also involve the defenses of their ego. It is my impression that these persons have a less rigidly established defense system and are able to exchange different kinds of defenses for each other, to drop certain defenses temporarily, or to employ more archaic defenses—a particular form of fluidity which permits them to keep more closely in touch with their unconscious than others are able to do.

the book represents to him his own creation, his way of self expression, this "love" may be rather of a narcissistic type. Moreover, the function as such—the acts of thinking and writing—may be a highly vested, preferred form of self satisfaction. After his work is published, its praise by the public, the splendid sale of the book, the gain of money from it, all these gratifications may be the writer's additional narcissistic rewards. But all these manifold narcissistic elements involved in such creative ego activity are bound to interfere with the function of thinking and writing if the major aim of the book does not remain the writer's true interest in the selected field, in the special material he deals with, in the discoveries he has made, or the ideas which he wants to develop: in short, an "objective" interest. The object-directed nature of his interest will find an expression in a quiet devotion to his work, to the point of self forgetfulness or even self sacrifice. In comparing personal object relations with social and cultural pursuits, we must, of course, admit that the latter ego activities are less "object-libidinal"; first, because they may be more "detached," i.e., cathected with more neutralized drives; but also because they permit and entice the individual to more narcissistic gratifications than mature love relations may commonly do.

Since all ego actions aim at gratification of the self on the outside (personal or inanimate) object, they represent at the same time object-related and narcissistic pursuits which must involve temporary changes in the cathexes of self and object representations and in the processes of discharge of self-directed as well as of object-directed (libidinal, aggressive, and neutralized) psychic energy. Normal ego functioning presupposes a sufficient, evenly distributed, enduring libidinal cathexis of both object and self representations. The action will arise from an initial hypercathexis of the specific object image and of the intended function with libidinal, aggressive, and neutralized energy. Besides, ego action requires the spur of a concomitant libidinal hypercathexis of the self representations, which will encourage and guarantee the success of the action. This libidinal cathexis extends to the representations, on the one hand, of the intended function, and of the body parts and organs to be employed for it, and, on the other hand, of the whole self as an entity. The rising cathexis of the latter manifests itself in general feelings of self confidence preceding and stimulating first the cathexis of the executive organs and then the action.

The increase of object cathexis puts the drive in motion, determines its direction, and leads, by way of drive-discharge processes, to completion of the action. In the course of successful actions, intense, rich feelings of identity are frequently experienced. After successful action, whatever excess libido is left is withdrawn from the object image and is turned back to other objects and to the self representations. Their rising cathexis finds expression in feelings of satisfaction in the body (or mental) parts used for the action, and in the general increase of self esteem. I may add that libidinal hypercathexis of the self representations, along with an aggressive hypercathexis of the object representations, is characteristic of narcissistic, aggressive, or sadistic attitudes toward the object; furthermore, that an insufficient libidinal object cathexis or an insufficient initial narcissistic cathexis may result in the partial inhibition of ego functions. A libidinal hypercathexis of the object—along with an aggressive hypercathexis of the self representations—is bound to produce failure, and corresponds to masochistic or self-destructive behavior. But a major withdrawal and shift of cathexis from the object representation to the self representation, such as occurs mostly in normal and pathological forms of regression, eventually leads to inactivity or to general inhibition of ego activity.

I shall conclude my discussion of the cathectic and discharge processes underlying ideational and functional ego activity by tracing out also their relation to the corresponding emotional expression. Affects and ideas, as I have previously stated, originate in physiological processes of discharge on the inside, which, with the opening up of the respective pathways, combine with processes of discharge to the outside. Both types of discharge lead at first only to sensations and concomitant primitive, prepatterned motor reactions; later on, they lead to full affectomotor manifestations associated with fantasies; eventually they lead to emotional experiences which attach themselves to fantasy and thought processes. These result in adequate motor activity with regard to objects and other autonomous ego functions.

My further inference, namely, that all ego activity, being satisfaction of the self on an object, must combine interrelated self- and object-directed (libidinal, aggressive, and neutralized) cathectic and drive-discharge processes, must be valid for emotional experience too. Being self expression as well as responses to outside stimuli, affects and feelings appear to be predominantly induced by and composed of both self-directed discharge on the inside and object-directed discharge toward the outside. With regard to the "turning of drives toward the self," I wish to stress that this drive vicissitude undergoes a decisive development as soon as self representations become established. From then on, the drive energy with which they are cathected can be discharged to the outside by way of thoughts, feelings, and motor actions which treat the self like an object. This development is of course greatly enhanced by the constitution of the superego which, as in the case of depression, can thus, e.g., effect the discharge of self-destructive energy by suicidal action. In view of this, self-destructive physiological phenomena must be regarded as more regressive than self-destructive thoughts, feelings, and actions.

The relations and proportions between self- and object-directed discharge processes have a high significance for the emotional qualities in general. Apart from the influence of the specific drives involved, these qualities appear indeed to be greatly determined by the part which discharge on the inside versus discharge toward the outside plays in the whole process inducing the affect. I need only refer to characteristic changes of the emotional qualities in the course of affective development when the child advances from the early pre-oedipal, narcissistic stage to the period at which true object-libidinal relations develop. No doubt these affective changes are the result of numerous influences. But quite apart from all these other factors, the early preoedipal affective organ language reflects the preponderance of internal physiological discharge processes at that stage. The colorful affect qualities and rapidly changing affects during the later preoedipal and early oedipal period, when the essentially self-expressive affectomotor activity of the child alternates with the most touching expression of object-related feelings, reflect his constant fluctuations between autistic-narcissistic and cling-ing-dependent attitudes toward the objects. Finally, the warm, affectionate feeling qualities and the rich feeling shades, which develop after establishment of stable self and object representations and of true object relations and ego activities, clearly betray the object-related nature and the changing proportions between self- and object-directed drive discharge and between libidinal, aggressive, and neutralized drive components in the emotional processes. These proportions appear to find a special reverberation in the qualitative differences between the affects of the autistic-schizoid personality type and of people who relate well to the object world. The wide and rich affective scale, the manifold and subtle shades of feeling, the warm and vivid emotional qualities in the latter point to the predominance of object libido and to the variety of its fusions with more or less neutralized energy. In contrast, the range of feelings in the former is limited mainly to certain affects, such as feelings of cold hostility, of anxiety, hurt, humiliation, of shame or pride, of security or insecurity, of high or low self esteem, of grandeur or inferiority and guilt. This and the affective coldness and rigidity of the autistic-schizoid personality appear to point to the prominent part of inhibited but unamalgamated aggression and the prevalence of self-directed emotional discharge processes.

Part II

Superego Formation and the Period of Latency

6

The Forestages of Superego Development

THE INTENSITY of the instinctual conflicts and the increasing structural differentiation during the oedipal period are reflected in the growing complexity of the identification processes which, under the influence of the oedipal taboos, undergo drastic modifications. Toward the end of this phase, they lead to the establishment of a new functional system, the superego, which gives all developmental processes an enormous impetus. Large amounts of psychic energy can now be liberated and utilized for aim-inhibited pursuits. From then on, the development of (nonsexual) physical activities, of social, intellectual, and cultural interests can make rapid progress. The latency period sets in.

It seems advisable to begin the discussion of the special identifications to which the superego owes its existence by pointing to at least some essential factors which determine the different qualities of the infantile identification processes. Their qualities depend on:

(1) The limitations of the child's own psychic organization (Spitz, 1957, p. 49);

(2) the sex, the personality, the attitudes and behavior of the objects and the qualities of the object's traits chosen for identification;

(3) the vicissitudes of the self and object representations

and the extent to which the child discovers and discerns the reality of his love objects and of his own self;

(4) hence, the degree to which the parental and other images serving for identification are close to the realistic models, become idealized, or may become removed from them or even reactively opposed to them;

(5) the degree to which independence of these objects is brought about by the identifications (Hartmann and Loewenstein, 1962);

(6) the qualities and aims of the drives and fantasies, and the experiences and perceptions inducing the identifications;

(7) the quality and vicissitudes of the underlying introjection and projection mechanisms;

(8) the degree to which the identifications serve defensive (or even restitutive) purposes, or develop as the pathological outcome of a neurotic or psychotic conflict.

With regard to these last factors, I mentioned above that not all infantile identifications arise under the influence of the child's sexual and ambivalence conflicts; that we can also observe identifications which, developing directly from the child's close intimacy with his love object, remain centered about it and hardly acquire any reactive or defensive qualities.

Quite a different variety of identifications originates in the child's indomitable competitive urges for sexual gratification and narcissistic expansion. They induce wishful fantasies of sexual identification with aggrandized images of his love objects, predominantly of his admired preoedipal and oedipal rivals. Such familiar fantasies acquire increasingly aggressive qualities to the extent to which the child rebels against instinctual frustration and narcissistic injuries and wants to break his symbiotic ties with the parents. Instinctual prohibitions and fears grant these sexual and aggressive identification fantasies only limited expression in the child's behavior. The sexual wishes undergo repression and recede, only to be revived, intensified, and acted out during the period of instinctual and narcissistic expansion in adolescence. But during childhood, in the wake of repression and ego maturation, the instinctual identifications with the parental love objects change their qualities, aims, and directions. Neutralizing and displacing the child's forbidden sexual, aggressive, and narcissistic strivings to acceptable aims and objects, they acquire entirely new, in part reactive and defensive qualities, and bring about remarkable modifications of the psychic structures. From then on they serve the building up of superego and ego and of aim-inhibited pursuits. The steering wheels for the ego identifications, which develop the child's attitudes, character traits, and behavior and promote his interests, pursuits, and achievements, are special types of identifications which lead to the establishment of inner goals and standards.

But we must realize that in the course of the oedipal period these specific identifications begin to move in two different directions, which are determined by the different vicissitudes of the child's wishful self and object images. I stressed that during the oedipal phase reality testing gains more and more momentum and promotes the child's distinction between his wishful imagery and more or less realistic representations of the object world and of his actual as well as his potential own self. Thus processes develop which advance under the influence of beginning superego development, but, above all, of ego maturation, of improving reality testing and self awareness, and of expanding functional ego activities. Gradually toning down the child's imagery to a much more realistic level, they modify the child's wishful aggrandized self images and transform them into ambitious but realistic object-directed goals by blending them with corresponding parental ego goals. Depending on the parents' personality, they may extend to all kinds of parental interests and attitudes, their ambitions and expectations with regard to the child's future. Thus they may involve such narcissistic aims as good appearance, physical, intellectual, vocational, financial, social success, and the like.

In his *New Introductory Lectures on Psychoanalysis,* Freud (1932) refers to the ego identifications with realistic parental images as contributing significantly to character formation and no longer influencing the superego, which has been determined by the earliest parental images. Since ego identifications presuppose a realistic evaluation of the parents, Freud regards them as formations arising on a much later developmental level than the superego identifications. I believe that such ego identifications with realistic parental images actually begin to develop in interaction with superego identifications. But after the infantile period of superego formation they certainly become increasingly important, and gain special significance in late adolescence with the modification and toning down of the superego codes during this period. Thus, at this stage, they actually appear to exercise a strong influence on the superego.

The child's ego goals and attainment standards, established with the support of such identifications with parental goals and achievement standards, become a forceful and useful steering wheel for the further development of the ego, as long as they involve truly object-directed ego interests and, in addition, become and remain subservient to the moral standards of the superego. However, as we shall see, in many persons they tend to maintain, as it were, a life of their own, and frequently harbor derivatives of intense aggressive-narcissistic strivings.

[92]

I shall come back to this issue in the discussion of shame and inferiority conflicts. Suffice it here to state that, closely interrelated with the identifications, which help to set up such realistic goals and achievement standards in the ego, we observe processes of a different nature which, serving primarily the solution of the child's instinctual conflicts, transform the primitive, wishful images of the self and the love objects into a unified ego ideal and, by internalization[1] of the parental moral prohibitions and demands, establish, to use Hartmann's and Loewenstein's terms, the "direction-giving," the "enforcing," and the "self-critical" superego functions.

Hartmann and Loewenstein (1962) stress "the fact that many inborn apparatus that serve the ego actually are of an inhibiting character" (p. 43). But they make the point that with respect to the superego as such it is better not to use the term maturation, and that "the autonomy" of the superego refers to its independence from the object and from the drives.

I may add that, in my opinion, superego formation is also determined by innate factors and that superego autonomy implies, in particular, freedom from pressures caused by early precursors of the superego. Hartmann and Loewenstein state that "Freud's theory allows us to include among the genetic determinants of 'conscience' also the history of the preoedipal vicissitudes of aggression" (p. 70). They mention, furthermore, that they do not regard it as unlikely that the direction-giving function of the superego works with a higher degree of neutralization than the enforcing functions.

I should like to enlarge upon these statements. I believe,

[1] Hartmann and Loewenstein (1962) speak of "internalization" if regulations which had taken place in interaction with the outside world are substituted for by inner regulations.

indeed, that in the development of the superego the pre-oedipal, the oedipal, and the adolescent vicissitudes of libido as well as aggression play a very influential part. Moreover, it is my impression that the direction-giving functions work with a higher degree of more or less neutralized libido than the "enforcing" functions which, as this very term indicates, seem to operate with a greater amount of aggression. What I want to stress is that, as in all kinds of psychic functions, the qualities of the different superego functions depend not only on the degree of neutralization but even more on the proportions between libido and aggression.

According to Hartmann and Loewenstein, the cruelty of the superego is expressive of an impairment of the ego's capacity for neutralization, i.e., of the impairment of an ego function. However, it seems to me that this capacity of the ego depends in turn on the preponderance of libidinal over aggressive forces. While I have repeatedly underscored the significance of this point for the building up of personal object relations and of (nonsexual) ego functions, I should like to stress here its importance for the establishment of sound superego functions.

However, in contrast to the ego, the superego, this unique human acquisition, becomes the one area in the psychic organization where, by virtue of a reactive reversal of aims, the child's grandiose wishful fantasies can find a safe refuge and can be maintained forever to the profit of the ego.

As I have already emphasized, Melanie Klein fails to distinguish the constitution of self and object representations, and of object relations and ego identifications, from superego formation. This fact appears to account for certain of her concepts which I believe to be erroneous. She does not clearly distinguish the establishment of object relations, which proceeds with the building up of self and object rep-

resentations in the ego, from the processes of partial identification with the love objects. These build up the ego and
eventually lead to superego formation. Consequently, she
dates the beginning of the latter back to the first months of
life.

In so far as these infantile, magic, wishful self and object
images begin to form the primitive kernel of an ego ideal
even before being fully separated, Melanie Klein is certainly
right. It is also true that at this early stage, love and identification can scarcely be differentiated; since the primitive
object relations entail the operation of continuous introjective and projective mechanisms, these processes are first in-
termingled. Moreover, we must certainly regard the first
pregenital reaction formations, which already begin to constitute internalized parental demands and prohibitions, as
forerunners of the superego.

However, even though the foundations of ego ideal and
superego are laid down during the first years of life, the
superego seems to arise as a definite psychic system only with
the passing of the oedipal conflicts. Evidently, its establishment presupposes that the psychosexual development and
the maturation of the ego have advanced to a certain level.
I shall return to this point. Let us first consider the preoedipal origins of the ego ideal and the precursors of the
superego.

The insufficient distinction between object and self during
the beginning constitution of an ego ideal, or rather of its
precursors, explains why in its deep, unconscious core we
may detect fusions of early infantile images of both the love
object and the self, and why at bottom the superego and the
ego ideal harbor the grandiose wishes of the preoedipal child
as well as his belief in the parental omnipotence. In fact,
parental demands and prohibitions probably can become

internalized only by joining forces with the child's own narcissistic, ambitious strivings to which, however, they give an entirely new direction.

In "On Narcissism: An Introduction," Freud (1914) refers to these origins of the ego ideal in early, narcissistic strivings when he says:

> That which he projects ahead of him as his ideal is merely his substitute for the lost narcissism of his childhood—the time when he was his own ideal [p. 51].

This double face of the ego ideal, which is forged from ideal concepts of the self and from idealized features of the love objects, gratifies indeed the infantile longing of which we said that it is never fully relinquished: the desire to be one with the love object. Even our never-ending struggle for oneness between ego and ego ideal reflects the enduring persistence of this desire.

I stated that the constitution of the superego system is prepared during the preoedipal stage by the development of the first reaction formations. In fact, the most drastic changes in the cathexis of the self and object representations are brought about, first, by the curbing of pregenital and sadistic strivings, then by the castration threat, and finally by superego formation.

Following up the various stages of superego formation, we shall have an opportunity to consider at least the most important influences of the instinctual vicissitudes on ego and superego development. Conflict-born and founded on countercathectic processes, the anal reaction formations for the first time turn the child's aggression drastically from his love object to his self. Contrary to the processes of sublimation which I discussed, reaction formations as such do not displace libido or aggression from forbidden onto aim-inhibited interests. Even though they certainly induce and reinforce the building up of such interests, they represent essentially changes in the child's attitudes toward his own instinctual strivings and in general toward himself, and consequently also toward the object world. Of course, changes in the child's attitudes are achieved not only by reaction formations. All forms of ego identifications lead to the development of characteristic, individual ego attitudes.

Let me clarify at this point what I mean by attitudes, or ego attitudes. We have so far scarcely considered their development, although they play such a prominent part in the building up of a person's character, of his individual personality, in short, of his identity. By attitudes we understand characteristic features which become manifest in the most general way in all mental areas: in a person's ideals and ideas, his feelings, and his behavior. When I said that reaction formations bring about changed attitudes, I meant that in a certain area a new principle begins to be effective in the child and to be divulged in his different feelings, ideas, and actions within this area. Thus, the reaction formations acquired during bowel training will show themselves first in ideas that feces are dirty and belong in the toilet and that children who soil are bad; second, in feelings of disgust at the bowels, of shame at loss of bowel control, of pride in achieving cleanliness and of pleasure in clean, neat, and beautiful things; and, third, in new aims and active efforts to move the bowels punctually on the toilet, to keep clean and to accept the meaning of time, the routine of life and schedules in general. In addition, aesthetic interests and the urge for artistic creation may develop, indicative of a beginning sublimation of anal drives. I need hardly mention that the reaction formations named above arise not only in con-

[97]

nection with bowel training but also have other roots and functions.

Even the responses of pity and compassion, which seemingly entail only feeling reactions or predispositions for such reactions, involve more than pure "feelings." They include not only an empathic understanding of suffering and ethical convictions, such as that people who suffer should be helped, but also a readiness actively to relieve their suffering.

Thus a good criterion for success or failure of reaction formations is frequently whether they have consistently changed the attitudes of a person. In neurotic pity there may be overwhelming feelings of pity, but no action; or exaggerated ideas of obligation or even helpful actions concerning those who suffer, but no true feelings, etc. (Jekels, 1930, 1936).

Infantile reaction formations establish the child's sense of human values in limited areas and change his earliest infantile value measures, a development which reaches a peak in the course of superego formation with the building up of a stable, moral value system.

The first infantile notions of what is valuable or worthless arise with the distinction made between pleasurable and unpleasurable oral experiences (in the broad sense of the term). Thus the earliest infantile value measures are those of pleasure versus unpleasure only. We can observe their reappearance in sad or happy states.

As oral deprivation alternates with gratification and these experiences become associated with the love object, images of a good and of a bad mother emerge, of a mother who may change from bad to good as frustration changes to gratification. When the child's aggressive reactions to frustration begin to arouse fears of retaliation, the "bad mother" will become a bad, punishing mother who may become reconciled by the child's being "good again." As we know, this emotional logic, not only of moral badness leading to punishment but of a pleasure premium inevitably attached to goodness, never ceases to be effective in the human mind and strongly influences the intrapsychic ego-superego relationship.

The child's conviction of such interrelations between the mother's and his own behavior is, of course, greatly reinforced by his training in cleanliness.

Since the learning of bowel control influences and even promotes anal erotism and infantile preoccupation with feces as part of the body, it contributes to the libidinal cathexis and to the child's awareness of his body self. At the same time, it intensifies his relationship to the mother and helps to teach the child that love involves not only receiving but giving.

In view of these manifold influences on the child's ego, the achievement of bowel control must thus be regarded as a very important step in his experience of ego independence and of mutual interrelations with his mother and, hence, in the development of his feelings of identity. But for the establishment of self-critical functions, the turning of aggression, and of a very particular form of aggression, toward the self has the greatest significance. What I refer to is a kind of aggression that aims at devaluation of the object and finds expression in depreciating, derogatory attitudes toward it. This form of aggression, which when turned onto the self is, as we know, predominant in depressive states, also plays a prominent role in normal development. It develops as the ubiquitous answer to infantile experiences of frustration, hurt, and disappointment, and has its origin in the infant's spitting or vomiting response to undesirable or unwanted food. This primitive, at first merely physiological response is

[99]

the forerunner of the feeling of disgust, a reaction formation which forever maintains close relations to pregenital, oral, and anal experiences. We frequently observe that, some time after being weaned, children begin to respond to the breast and to mother's milk, or to milk in general, with intense disgust.

In the course of the training in cleanliness such derogatory, aggressive reactions become displaced from the oral to the anal zone; bad food, vomit, feces become associated with each other. From then on, anal aggression and its derivatives will always be used as expressions of profound depreciation.

But disgust, originally a derogatory reaction to the frustrating breast, i.e., to an outside object, now becomes a response to the child's own body part, the feces, and to his own bad behavior. Very ambivalent attitudes toward the anus and feces develop as what had been his most valuable present to the mother becomes more and more an object of disgust and derogation.

Feelings of disgust and shame, a reaction formation to exhibitionistic wishes, from now on assist the child in his struggle with his forbidden pregenital and, later on, genital wishes. His reaction to his own "good" or "bad" anal behavior, his pride in successful bowel training, his pleasure in giving the anal present to his mother, his shame and disgust at losing bowel control, all these reactions indicate remarkable changes in the child's attitudes and in his concepts of value or worthlessness.

In the modifications of infantile value measures one can rather clearly distinguish those which come about under the influence of standards conveyed by education and are supposed to achieve instinctual control and inhibition, from those which are connected with the development of the child's narcissistic strivings and his autonomous ego functions.

The educational influences on the development of the infantile value system find expression mainly in the advance of tension tolerance and the acceptance, first of the sphincter morale, then of standards for social behavior, and eventually of general ethical codes whose core is the incest taboo and the law against parenticide.

The modifications of the infantile conceptions of value caused by the changing vicissitudes of infantile narcissism and advancing ego development announce themselves during the preoedipal, anal-sadistic period in the predominance of magic ideas and feelings, such as discussed previously. They are centered about the high value of omnipotence.

Of course, the magic fantasy life of the child at the pre-oedipal stage finds a large playground in the oral and anal areas. This becomes manifest in the child's omnipotent ideas about the maternal breast and his own feces, in his attempts to assert his power either by soiling or by withholding feces. His continuing tendency to regard the mother as an extension of himself will come to the fore in fantasies that his feces belong to and are part of his mother, just as her breast belongs to him.

The child's intense preoccupation with such omnipotent ideas and strivings during this period indicates indeed that, quite apart from the establishment of frustration tolerance and sphincter morale, the original equation of value with pleasure is losing ground in favor of a new concept of value, that of strength versus weakness.

In fact, during the preoedipal and increasingly during the oedipal stage the child begins to develop more realistic notions of the value of power and strength. Centered about his wishes for instinctual (oral, anal, urinary) control and mastery and for physical (phallic) strength and skills, they arise in connection with his growing independent ego achievements and gradually replace his magic fantasies of omnipotence. These new notions of the value of power and strength find expression in visible experiences of pride and superiority in reaction to actual accomplishments, or in experiences of shame, disgust, and feelings of inadequacy in response to actual failures. It is my impression that manifestations of pride in new attainments can be observed even earlier than shame reactions and develop, in part, independently of the child's instinctual conflicts and the mother's attitudes and reactions.

Of course, the realization of the actual value of power and strength also changes the child's attitudes to his love objects. While the child's first images of a "good" or "bad" mother had only referred to a gratifying or depriving mother, good and bad now assume a different meaning. His notion of a worthy parent will express his increasing need for a consistently strong mother or father, respectively.

This transformation is indicative of the child's narcissistic expansion and his advancing ego formation: of the increasing cathexis of the self representations and his bodily and mental functions, and of the child's growing awareness of the self as an entity, i.e., of his identity. But it is even more a repercussion of the child's clearer realization of his psychobiological dependency on the parents. It evidences his need for their further support in the building up of his ego, his need for powerful parental images with which he can identify. This explains why the child can tolerate frustration, deprivation, and even severe aggression and profound narcissistic hurt and constriction by the mother better than her weakness or her loss.

This is of particular importance in the development of

masochists and of persons with identity problems. From such cases we learn that a helpless child with a hostile, rejecting, or smothering mother will do his best to accept and submit to his powerful, aggressive love object, and even give up his own self rather than give up the love object entirely.

But even normally the vanishing belief in his own omnipotence will teach the child to prefer security to pleasure and hence to accept a strong love object that gives him security and guidance, even though it may deprive him of pleasure and freedom.

Whereas the pregenital notions of strength still revolve mainly about maternal power and security represented by oral-anal property (breast-feces), these ideas during the oedipal period become attached to the penis as the precious symbol of phallic strength. They find expression in the child's admiration of his father's powerful genital, which is coveted because it appears to account for the mother's preference of the father. The final renunciation of the infantile genital strivings and the acceptance of the incest taboo and of the law against patricide can be achieved because the child's wishes for phallic intactness eventually defeat his genital cravings. In this way a solution of the oedipal conflicts is brought about.

The prevailing fears and notions of danger during the various infantile stages reverberate the changes of the infantile scales of value just described. In the course of the preoedipal period, the child's earliest fears of separation and loss of pleasure change, on the one hand, to fears of loss of the powerful, supportive, and protective love objects or of their love, respectively, and, on the other hand, to fears of loss of his powerful, priceless property, the bowels. Around these central fears are grouped the fears derived from his first reaction formation: fears of being exposed or disgraced, of being despised and rejected. During the oedipal period fear becomes centered about the precious genital organ; it is castration fear. As we shall see, derivatives of these preoedipal and oedipal fears and of the scales of value on which they rest partly survive in the adult ego, and find expression in his ego goals and pursuits and in corresponding narcissistic conflicts. But with superego formation, with the internalization of general ethical and moral commands and standards, the castration fears become, in part, transformed into fears of the superego, of not measuring up to the standards of the ego ideal.

Before we can approach the processes of identification which ultimately lead to the establishment of a new psychic system, we must scrutinize once more the influence of frustration and disappointment, of narcissistic hurt and narcissistic constriction on the development of this system, and on the child's self esteem and self feelings.

I have underscored the great contribution that such experiences can make to the building up of the system ego and the child's object relations, provided that he is brought up in a general atmosphere of love and security. But if such frustrating experiences are severe, begin at an early developmental stage, and are insufficiently compensated by parental love and empathy, they may create dangerous ambivalence conflicts. Their effects on the constitution of object relations and identifications have already been discussed.

In the beginning, the child goes only through fleeting, though repeated, experiences of frustration, which are not yet associated with the love object. Only with the establishment of object relations do they turn into experiences of being hurt and disappointed in the parents as human entities.

I should like to revert here to my remarks on the child's reaction of devaluation. Fleeting at first as the frustration by which they are provoked, such reactions cannot find expression in feelings and thoughts before vague notions of value have developed. Arising for the first time during the anal-sadistic period, such unconscious and conscious derogatory and disdainful thoughts, feelings, and impulses concerning the parents increase and expand under the impact of oedipal conflicts and of the discovery of the difference of sexes, particularly if the child should also gain information about his parents' sexual activities.

Oral, anal, and genital forms of aggressive devaluation combine, and the child may experience his degraded love objects either as weak and empty, or as dirty and disgusting, or as destroyed and castrated.

The total effect of his disheartening experiences is a "disillusionment" (*Enttäuschung,* the German term for disappointment), which normally has a beneficial, double influence. Promoting the child's testing of external and of his own internal reality, it assists him, as I previously pointed out, in gradually relinquishing his illusions, i.e., his magic fantasies about his love objects and himself. At the same time, however, it is the main incentive for the child's increasing idealization of his parents, because it stimulates the development of strong, reactive libidinal strivings.

However, when disillusionment is experienced before the child is ready to fight his hostile devaluation of the parents with the support of idealizations, it may arrest the advance of object relations and interfere with normal ego-ideal and superego formation, which depend on the child's admiration and respect for his parents. This may turn the child into a "cynic" with preponderantly "selfish"-infantile ego goals and a defective superego which has no control over them. Moreover, as long as the boundaries between self and object are still indistinct, and libidinal and aggressive forces freely

[105]

move back and forth between self and object images, disappointment and devaluation of objects will impart themselves immediately to the self and cause self devaluation and narcissistic hurt; and, conversely, narcissistic injuries will induce devaluation of the love objects and disappointment in them.

The reactions of normal children to the castration shock, certainly one of the most traumatic infantile experiences, highlights this combination and interrelationship of infantile disappointment and narcissistic hurt. In addition, they very clearly demonstrate the favorable and unfavorable effects of disillusioning infantile experiences.

As Freud (1931) pointed out, the female castration conflict is already induced during the preoedipal period by the little girl's disappointment that her mother did not provide her with a penis. In the little boy, the effect of his discovery of his mother's supposedly castrated genital appears to depend largely on the severity of his preoedipal disappointments in his mother. This is also true for the little girl.

In a normal child the realization of the differences between the sexes certainly arouses his curiosity and spirit of investigation, promotes his inquisitive detection of the external world, and helps to displace libidinal and aggressive strivings onto the sense of perception and onto critical, intellectual activity. In general, if the hostility released by such experiences can be sufficiently absorbed and utilized by the ego, the function of reality testing profits greatly. Critical and self-critical functions are stimulated, the realistic perceptions of the world and of the self expand and sharpen, and the ability of the ego to tone down illusory concepts and expectations becomes reinforced in turn.

In this process the little girl fails, of course, more easily. Since for both sexes phallic strength remains for a long time the outstanding symbol of power and value, her feelings of narcissistic injury induce fantasies of having been castrated by mother because of masturbation. To make matters worse, her disappointment and supposed deprivation result not only in feelings of being rejected by her mother because of her deficiency but also in a profound depreciation of the castrated mother and of her own, castrated self. From these reactions the little girl recovers very slowly.

In fact, the castration conflict complicates the little girl's development of object relations as profoundly as the vicissitudes of her narcissism. Ultimately, though, women may have more complex but not necessarily more severe narcissistic conflicts and more disturbed object relations than men.

The little boy is usually less severely affected by the discovery of the supposed female castration. Although it confirms and reinforces his own castration fears, his oedipal attachment normally supports his recovery from the trauma of the castration shock.

I have previously asserted that the discovery of the sexual differences is a milestone in male development, in so far as it signifies the onset of consistent identifications with the father, identifications founded on masculine equality. The castration shock will cause the little boy, indeed, to turn both admiration and envy definitely away from his mother to his glorious, phallic father and to make him the protector, supporter, model, and powerful extension of his self.

The little boy's common reaction to the "castrated" mother—his self assertion as a superior male like his father toward the weaker female—is worth mentioning again, because this device becomes a well-known general pattern of establishing superiority over a disappointing object.

On the other hand, the little boy may react as the little girl commonly does, but only for a limited period. We see this only when he has early been exposed to severe disappointment in the mother and suffered narcissistic injuries. In this case he may devaluate his mother to the point of giving her up altogether as a love object, identify with the castrated female, and select the father as his main love object for the purpose of getting his big penis.

Such impressive cases as well as the vicissitudes of the female castration conflict clearly demonstrate the fatal influence which early disappointment and narcissistic injuries may have on self esteem and the identity feelings. However, these can be studied even better in prepsychotic patients, precisely because their pathology may bring the essential points into relief. But I cannot deal with this issue before I have discussed the shame and guilt conflicts. I shall presently turn to the establishment of that outstanding new psychic system which achieves a solution of the sexual and aggressive infantile conflicts and serves to prevent the growth of such inner processes as might lead to a harmful devaluation or even "inner" loss of the oedipal love objects and of the self.

7

The Idealization of the Love Objects, Ego-Ideal Formation, and the Development of Superego Identifications

THE CHILD'S efforts to overcome his dangerous sexual and aggressive tendencies toward his parents find assistance in reactively intensified opposite strivings: his admiration and overestimation of his parents, and his magic belief in their omnipotence and high value. It is significant that this inflation of the parental images during the preoedipal and early oedipal phases is still mainly caused by the dependent child's need for powerful parents. Expressive of his own aggressive-narcissistic demands, it thus leads at first only to aggrandizements and glorifications of his love objects—fantasies which give him security, expand his self image, and raise his own self esteem. But under the influence of education and of advancing instinctual repression and inhibition, the child's notions of value progress further. His endeavors to master pregenital and phallic narcissistic-sadistic impulses and hostile-derogatory attitudes are aided by reactive libidinal strivings. Gradually he constructs moral and ethical codes and standards, which begin to outweigh the values of eternal pleasure and gratification, of property and of physical or mental power and strength. Thus, the child's earlier tendency to aggrandize and glorify the parents—and himself—will gradually become modified and transformed into a tendency toward a true idealization of the parental love objects.

In his paper on narcissism Freud (1914) advised analysts to distinguish carefully between such idealizations which involve objects and the processes of sublimation, which influence the direction of the child's own strivings. I may additionally point to the distinction and the interrelations between both these processes and the reaction formations. Reaction formations accomplish changes in the child's attitudes toward his own and toward instinctual strivings in general. Sublimations, enhanced by the reaction formations, displace psychic energy from instinctual goals onto other, aim-inhibited, interests. Both processes are interwoven with the glorification or idealization of the parental love objects and are influenced by it. When superego formation has set in, this idealization begins to be extended from the idealized persons to abstract values in general, to ideas, ideals, and ideal pursuits.

The originally weak boundaries and cathectic vacillations between self and object images in the small child tend to cast the glorification and idealization back from the love object to the self. As the setting up of idealized parental images protects the child from his aggressive devaluation of the parents, the constitution, first of wishful aggrandized, then of idealized self images counteracts the infantile tendency toward rapid self devaluation.

Thus the processes of idealization not only serve to protect infantile object relations, which are threatened by the child's sexual desires and his ambivalence, but also help to heal the narcissistic wounds. Forever close to magic imagery and yet indispensable to the ego, the ego ideal is eventually molded from such idealized object and self images.

The separate though concomitant building up of an ego

ideal, composed of idealized parental and self images and of realistic ego goals as well as realistic self and object representations, appears to reflect the child's simultaneous acceptance of the reality principle and his resistance to it. Whereas part of himself, the ego that is in continuous contact with reality, gradually tones down illusions and accepts reality, another part of the self, that cannot cease to believe in magic, is split off. However, this may only promote a survival of magic images and conceptions in the id rather than their transformation into internalized ideals, moral codes, and ethical standards for the ego.

This is accomplished by virtue of special identifications, the superego identifications. I have previously stressed the role of reality testing in the establishment of reality-directed ego goals. I must now re-emphasize the point that the ability to build up superego identifications, i.e., to accept and internalize the moral standards, the moral directives, and the moral criticism handed down by the parents, depends likewise on the advancing maturation of the ego. The latter promotes not only the distinction between the real parents and their idealized images but also the gradual transformation of such images into an abstract ego ideal. This process, discussed more extensively in the next chapter, brings about a compromise between irrational desires and the demands of reality. It permits the survival of magic, idealized self and object images, as abstract conceptions of the human being that we may wish to be like and may endeavor to become, even though we may never achieve such a goal. The prominent, strange, and precious quality of the ego ideal is its unreality and its distance from the real self. Although we are ordinarily perfectly aware of this, the ego ideal exerts a tremendous influence on our realistic behavior.

The vicissitudes of the ego ideal reflect, of course, the

development of infantile value measures. Its deep unconscious core harbors derivatives of early notions of value, such
as the idea of eternal happiness, of glamour and wealth, or
physical and mental power and strength; notions which do
not yet have the quality of moral ideals but, partly surviving
in our ego goals, may play a paramount role in patients whose
superego has never matured.

But the construction of the superego rests not only on the
process of ego-ideal formation. Interwoven with it, identifications develop which, using especially acoustic pathways
(Isakower, 1939), internalize the daily parental demands and
prohibitions, the dos and don'ts, the approvals and disap-
provals expressed by the parents and other parental figures
who, as Freud pointed out, hand down their own superego
codes to the child. These processes develop the self-critical
functions and the "enforcing" qualities of the moral demands
of the superego. Subsequently, the building up of the ego,
in general, advances under the control of the parents as
well as of the superego. From then on, the ego identifications,
too, no longer aim merely at likeness with external objects
but also at likeness with internalized standards.

Freud has repeatedly referred to the rather defective development of the superego, to its lack of independence and
stability in women. It is certainly true that many women, as
Sachs (1928) so beautifully demonstrated, tend to attach their
ego ideal to their partner and to accept his views and ideas
as their own. However, in general, Freud's opinion on this
issue appears somewhat biased by his conviction that women,
already feeling castrated, lack the most important incentive
for superego formation: the castration fear.

From my clinical experiences with female patients, both
adult and children, I have derived the definite impression

[112]

that the female superego is not defective but different in nature from the male superego. I actually believe that because of the early onset of her castration conflict the little girl develops the nucleus of a true ego ideal even earlier than the little boy (Jacobson, 1937). Since the idea of her castration is quite unacceptable, the little girl first responds to her discovery of the sexual differences with persistent attempts at denial of her supposed deficiency. During this prolonged period she suffers from intense castration fears which only gradually yield to the discouraging conviction of having been really castrated and to aggressive impulses to recover the lost phallus. The more these notions gain in strength, the greater becomes the little girl's depreciation of her mother and of herself. Eventually, her preoedipal disappointment and devaluation of her mother's and her own deficient genital lead to a rejection of her mother as a sexual love object—in favor of the phallic father. Quite commonly, the result is a premature relinquishment of genital activities, with withdrawal and shift of narcissistic libido from the genital to the whole body. My case material has left no doubt that these serious conflicts, and in particular the dangers arising from the little girl's self deflation and the devaluation of her mother, are mastered by the early establishment of a maternal ego ideal, though of a very immature one: the ideal of an unaggressive, clean, neat little girl who is determined to renounce sexual activities. The building up of this early ego ideal is commonly combined with the establishment of a feminine-narcissistic goal which will gain great importance in the little girl's future: the attainment of physical attractiveness.

Frequently we can observe that the female ego ideal absorbs and forever replaces the "illusory penis" fantasy. Women of this type usually deny any masculine tendencies or penis envy but display instead an uncommon narcissistic pride in their "inner values," their moral integrity, the high level of their standards, the relentless strength of their ideals; values which turn out unconsciously to represent their "inner penis."

But the further maturation of the ego ideal and the setting up of more advanced superego standards in the little girl are frequently disrupted as her persistent wishes for recovery of her penis are turned toward her father. Because of its origin in her castration conflicts, the little girl's oedipal attachment to the father appears to activate regressive processes. They retransform to some extent those introjective mechanisms which constituted the precocious ego ideal into fantasies of oral and genital incorporation centered about the paternal phallus. Such regressive reactions inhibit and delay the establishment of an independent ego as well as the further internalization, depersonification, and abstraction of ethical codes in the little girl and lead to a reattachment of her wishful self image to an outside person: to the glamorous figure of her phallic father. Freud was certainly correct in stating that in woman the leading fear is not fear of castration but of loss of love; however, during this phase of her oedipal conflict, loss of her father's love represents also a narcissistic injury: the loss of her—i.e., her father's—penis.

The experience of oedipal love and disappointment, supported by the biological increase of heterosexual strivings and of sexual rivalry with the mother, again influences the development of the little girl's identifications in a feminine direction. The final outcome of her conflict depends a great deal on the father's attitudes and on the mother's personality and love. On the whole, I believe that the eventual constitution of a self-reliant ego, and of a mature ego ideal and autonomous superego in women is all the more successful the better the little girl learns to accept her femininity and thus can find her way back to maternal ego and superego identifications.

In *The Ego and the Id* Freud (1923) began his discussion of ego and superego identification with a reference to depressive identifications, without further clarifying the differences between the former and the latter. In studying Freud's chapter on the ego and the superego, we notice certain discrepancies. On the one hand, Freud refers to the probability of simultaneous object relations and identifications with the love object. On the other hand, he asserts that the little boy's relations to his father originate in his identification with him. And at the same time he finds it puzzling that the ego and superego identifications of the little boy are centered about the figure of the father rather than that of the mother. Since Freud believed that identifications, as in melancholia, usually arise from the renunciation of the love object, which for the little boy is mainly the mother, he concluded that we should expect him to identify in the first place with his mother. Freud resolved this problem by pointing to the bisexuality of the child, to the necessity of overcoming both his heterosexual and homosexual strivings and, on the other hand, to the influence of the little boy's constitutionally preponderant masculinity on his identifications. I believe we need not even resort to the child's bisexuality for an understanding of the child's stronger identification with his oedipal rival, though this identification is certainly apt to resolve his homosexual problem.

Freud's reference to the identifications in melancholia was certainly very meaningful, inasmuch as it called attention to the role of the child's oedipal renunciation in the constitution of superego identifications. But we must realize that the child does not actually lose his oedipal love object. He must

[115]

give up his incestuous and patricidal wishes in favor of affectionate attachments to his parents. And the most striking analogy between the melancholic and the child is that the child's strongest incentive for idealization and superego identifications is the danger of "inner" object loss. This danger arises less from his love relationship to the incestuous object than from his severe ambivalence toward his oedipal rival and his greater narcissistic dependence on this revered figure.

Whereas Freud emphasized the fact that the boy's relationship to his mother is primarily of the anaclitic type, we must admit that because of the child's early infantile symbiotic relationship with the mother, she is for both male and female child the first object of love as well as of primitive identifications. I have shown that this begins to be altered by the rising rivalry conflicts and that it changes definitely as soon as the sexual differences are discovered. From that time on, the father's genital is admired and coveted by both boy and girl. We remember the little girl's complication: her identifications with the mother can assert themselves only to the extent to which her rivalry and her phallic identification with the father yield to a true love relationship with him. Evidently her narcissistic hurt, the supposed castration, and her tremendous envy and admiration of phallic strength have even more weight for some time than her constitutional heterosexuality.

Thus we must conclude that the child's narcissistic-dependent and competitive-aggressive strivings exercise from the beginning a decisive, or perhaps the greatest, influence on the direction and choice of his ego and superego identifications; furthermore, in both sexes, these strivings, at first centered about the omnipotent (breast-phallus) mother, soon become attached to the powerful, phallic father, but in the little girl eventually return to the mother. Moreover, my previous discussion laid special emphasis on the solution of the ambivalence conflict by ego-ideal and superego formation, a conflict which is also the force behind the pathological superego identifications in melancholics. Since the normal little boy's hostility is much greater toward his father than toward his mother, the paternal image tends to become reactively more idealized than that of the mother. In fact, extreme idealization of women, which Freud considers a characteristically masculine attitude, can, in my experience, be observed more frequently in men who have strong unconscious feminine identifications.

These considerations explain why the male superego bears mainly the impact of paternal influences, and the female superego partly that of paternal and eventually predominantly of maternal influences.

Both normal and pathological identifications may be induced by fear of losing a love object that serves as a source of narcissistic support, and may aim at preserving this object by processes of introjection. However, the influence of psychotic identifications on the drive cathexes of self and object representations is quite the opposite of that of normal ego and superego identifications. In the course of the latter, the object relations to the parents gain in strength and stability by a decrease of sexual and aggressive components, with concomitantly growing ability to maintain a steady level of self esteem, independent of narcissistic supply from without. The libidinal cathexis of the love-object representations becomes reduced, but above all it changes its quality. Apart from parental love, which is, of course, the best guarantee for a sound development of object relations and self esteem, the latter finds a particular stronghold in the processes of superego identifications. It does so on the one hand in the processes of idealization and ego-ideal formation, which stimulate ego development and effectively resist and counteract both self devaluation and devaluation of the parents, and on the other hand in the turning of more or less neutralized libido and aggression toward the self by development of the direction-giving, the enforcing, and the self-critical superego functions which are utilized by the ego.

Psychotic identifications, caused by the fury of ambivalence conflicts, arise from the breakdown of ego functions and object relations and replace these relations (Jacobson, 1954b). Normal idealizations, ego-ideal formation, ego and superego identifications are founded on a successful, reactive strengthening of the libidinal forces.

I can now supplement my previous statements concerning the cathectic shifts connected with the development of aim-inhibited ego interests. I may add that simultaneously, and interrelated with these processes, the ego ideal comes into existence by being endowed with libido that had originally been vested in the child's wishful self and object images. Regarding the superego as a system, it would not be precise to say that it becomes cathected with libidinal and aggressive forces. The best way to define the cathectic conditions might be to say that, with the development of superego functions, the self representations will become cathected with libidinal, aggressive, and neutralized energies, which, formerly a part of the ego, are now at the disposal of the superego.

Arising with the renunciation of libidinal and aggressive strivings toward the oedipal love objects, the superego identifications permit a large amount of the libido and aggression which had been so exclusively centered about these objects to be absorbed by ego and superego and their functions, and by the ego's defense system.

[118]

8

The Organization and Integration of Different Superego Components into a Consolidated Functional System

Wᴇ ᴋɴᴏw that the development of an effective defense organization in the ego depends on the acceptance and internalization of the moral codes and standards conveyed by the parents. This is a slow process. It begins with the acceptance of "sphincter morality." But only at the end of the oedipal phase have the building up, the integration, and organization of superego identifications proceeded far enough to create firm moral codes. Centered about the incest taboo and the law against patricide, they begin at this stage to become independent of the parents and to displace the conflicts between parents and child onto the inner, mental stage. Then only can we observe a gradual depersonification and abstraction of the ego ideal, combined with the development of consistently demanding, directive, prohibitive, and self-critical superego functions. This is the stage at which the superego comes into existence as a new specific functional system, which replaces—at least partly—castration fear with a new danger signal: with fear of the superego. In its establishment, the child's renunciation of infantile sexuality and of his sexual competition with the parental rival finds special expression in the gradual removal of the codes, fears, and criticism of the superego from the parents as persons. This process gains tremendous momentum from the intensification of affectionate bonds with the parents and the increasing drive neutralization, which are indicative of the advancing ego development and in turn give the latter strong support. Patients who were unable to ward off their infantile incestuous and aggressive desires by virtue of stable defenses suffer from an invasion of unattenuated sexual and aggressive impulses into the ego and superego, which is evidence of insufficient drive neutralization. Such patients also regularly show a personification of the superego, which can hardly be distinguished from wishful magic object and self images, and therefore tends to be reprojected on outside persons. In such cases the ego-superego relationship remains at a personified sadomasochistic level. This points again to the role of ego maturation in the development of the superego and leads to the question: precisely what are the factors which are actually responsible for the formation of a special system at this particular time?

Of course, our answers could resort to Freud's statements concerning the incentives to superego formation. This is the period at which the instinctual conflicts of the child come to a dangerous climax; when his fears are of an intensity and power never previously reached, because they refer to the threat of castration; hence, when sexual renunciation concerning the incestuous love object is enforced with absolute finality which by far surpasses the restrictions imposed on the child's pregenital drive components.

However, can the enormous impact of castration fear be regarded as the main incentive to the formation of the superego? It is true, we can hardly imagine a more powerful instrument to enforce the acceptance of the parental standards than the castration threat.

[120]

But I should like to play the devil's advocate for a moment. Let us remember that conflicts between ego and superego may become so unbearable that they cause a re-externalization of the superego, its reattachment to the external world. Why then should intense castration fear cause the infantile psychic organization to burden itself with the building up of a system which substitutes for fear of criticism, threats, and punishment from without an even more painful endopsychic type of anxious tension? This objection is of value, at least in so far as it calls attention to the different nature of castration fears and guilt feelings.

To begin with, castration fears, though signaling external danger, are not primarily induced by threats from without. They originate in the child's own sadistic castration wishes which are attributed to the parental images and then ascribed to—and possibly confirmed by—the real objects.

Thus, inasmuch as castration fears are magic retaliation fears of threatening parental images, they arise, likewise, from endopsychic tensions. The difference is that castration fear develops within the ego as a result of conflicts between ego and id, whereas superego fear is expressive of conflicts between superego and ego. The normal ego can probably deal better with this intersystemic conflict; all the more so since the superego develops into a complex functional system, and superego pressure becomes manifest not only in anxiety, i.e., in fear of the superego, but in a special, new type of painful experience which we call guilt feeling. Comparing these two affective responses, we realize that with regard to their nature, quality, content, and function, guilt feelings are quite different from castration fears. In the latter the rather ferocious qualities of the earliest infantile imagery seem to survive, even though their content is determined by the genital nature of the oedipal strivings. In general, the parental images at the oedipal stage give evidence of remarkable changes and revisions when compared with the early infantile imagery. The child at the age of four or five has already found his way to more realistic notions of kindly guiding, loving, rewarding, but also angry, demanding, critical, punishing parents. But castration fears are unequivocally irrational fears of threatening parental images; reflecting the boundless cruelty of the small child, they belong to a type of imagery which is actually on a much earlier infantile level than the child's object images at this phase in general. By becoming toned down, however, they develop into effective warning signals, which strictly enforce the incest taboo by virtue of repression and other auxiliary defense mechanisms. But, being what they are, they speak a singularly primitive moral language. They do not give any special direction, and have no link with those guiding parental images and reaction formations which I have discussed and which already during the preoedipal stage gain influence on the ego and encourage social behavior, functional ego activity, and sublimations.

However, as "the heir of the Oedipus complex," the superego seems to come to life as a system that takes over the signal function of castration fear, yet combines it effectively with such guiding and self-critical functions which are a safeguard against castration, since they offer definite directions as to how to prevent punishment. On what premises and under what circumstances does this come to pass?

Are the decisive factors the renunciation of the incestuous desires and of the castration and death wishes against the oedipal rival? Probably this renunciation succeeds only with the support of those identifications which result in superego formation. I have asserted that this could not be accomplished without increasing reactive idealization of the parents and that it certainly accounts for intensified processes of identification with idealized parental images during the oedipal period. But why should this not simply lead to special processes of identification in the ego? Why should it bring about the formation of a new functional unit that is part of the ego, yet set apart from it?

We may question whether the decision to delineate this particular area from the ego and call it the superego is not actually an arbitrary one. For several reasons I cannot share this opinion. First of all, Freud's final systemic distinctions are based on significant inner experiences. It is not accidental that in times of conflict we may hear the voice of temptation, the id; the voice of reason, the ego; and the voice of conscience, the superego. Evidently, we experience the superego as a distinctly separate inner institution, because it represents a definite functional unit.

I have already described processes which occur during the preoedipal stage, especially in the little girl, which result in the constitution of a primitive ego ideal without as yet creating a functionally efficient inner moral agency.

This has been stressed especially by A. Reich (1954) and also by Piers and Singer (1953), who regard the ego ideal, in general, as an earlier formation. Inasmuch as identifications, first with aggrandized and then with idealized parental images, are only part of the superego development but do not in themselves lead to system formation, I share this opinion. It was stressed that superego formation is a gradual, complex process which has preoedipal forestages; and that the preoedipal ego ideal is but one among many superego precursors. Like other such forerunners, it is at first primitive in nature; as it passes through the various developmental stages it matures and, joining the other superego components, eventually becomes a significant part of the whole system.

[123]

Considering that superego fear preserves castration fear, we realize that the threatening parental images which induce the latter must be likewise regarded as superego precursors that develop, change their content and quality, and become integrated into this system. The preoedipal forerunners of the superego call, indeed, on a very wide range of parental and self images, which we may again bring to mind.

On the one hand, there is the archaic imagery of which we have just spoken in reference to castration fears; imagery derived from the child's own instinctual strivings which induce irrational, physical retaliation fears (of being bitten or devoured, of being robbed of body content and, later, of being castrated). On the other hand, there is imagery more closely related to reality, to verbally expressed parental prohibitions and demands; this imagery arouses fears and expectations first at a primitive, then at a more advanced emotional level (fears of separation and loss of the object, of abandonment and of loss of love, fears of disapproval, exposure, rejection, criticism; expectations of love, approval, rewards). These notions reflect the child's varying ambivalent feelings and the parents' emotional responses and educational attitudes. They not only provoke fears but already offer positive incentives and directives for pregenital reaction formations and sublimations, and lead to internalization of certain behavior standards. And, finally, there is the imagery derived from the child's narcissistic, omnipotent, and eventually moral-perfectionistic strivings: the idealized object and self images from which the ego ideal, the moral guide of the ego, is coined.

My summary of these three types of imagery and my distinction between them were intentionally schematic and simplified. I wanted to emphasize that in its preoedipal forestages the superego—or what will become the superego—

still consists only of rather disconnected components originating in self and object imagery of different instinctual and ego stages and levels. They partly relate to each other. They partly even collaborate. They have in part the character of approving or disapproving, guiding or threatening object images and in part that of wishful self images. Here and there they already begin to merge and to assume the character of compelling inner standards. However, they lack maturity, uniformity, coherence. They serve many masters, but are not yet a masterful, organized functional unit, a system in its own right.

Evidently the psychic organization is not ready to build up the superego as a functional system before the maturation of the ego and of object relations has progressed to a certain level.[1] I refer to the development of feeling and thought processes, of perception and reality testing, of logical and abstract thinking, of the sense of time, of critical judgment and discrimination, and finally to the development of self and object representations, of affectionate object relations, of ego identifications and of the executive functions of the ego.

What enables the psychic organization toward the end of the oedipal phase to constitute the superego as a system is, I believe, the rapid advance of ego development, with structural ego modifications and changes in the nature of object relations and identifications accomplished by the oedipal defense struggle. Thus we can say that the superego comes into being as a system only after and because castration fear

---

[1] In his paper on "Vicissitudes of Superego Functions and Superego Precursors in Childhood," Beres (1958) likewise emphasizes the influence of ego maturation on superego formation. The same point was carefully examined and illuminated by Dr. Stanley A. Leavy in an as yet unpublished paper on "Speech, Acting Out, and Superego Formation," presented in a clinical discussion group a number of years ago.

has helped the ego to accomplish at least a partial mastery of the oedipal conflicts. It propels the development of the ego, of affectionate object relations, of self and object constancy, and of general drive neutralization to the point where the specific type of identification processes can set in which constitute an effective functional superego system. The superego will then, in turn, achieve the final solution of the incestuous problem and further promote the process of ego maturation, the growth and organization of personal relations and identifications, and the establishment of a solid defense system.

The development of the above-mentioned ego faculties to a certain level is indeed needed, because superego formation appears to presuppose an advance of the ego from the stage of concretistic object and self imagery to that of a more conceptual, abstract, and discriminating understanding of the parental personalities; an understanding of their mental characteristics, their superego standards, their ideas and opinions, their attitudes and wishes, their expectations and demands as well as their prohibitions, and of the consistency of the moral codes which they imply. To the extent to which this conceptual and emotional understanding develops, the imagistic components in which the superego originates will mature, change with regard to their content, and assume abstract qualities. Only at this stage can selected ideal, directive, prohibitive, disapproving, and approving parental traits and attitudes and parental teachings become constructively correlated and gradually blended into a consistent, organized set of notions.

This developmental process extends to the end of adolescence and even further. In its course the introjective mechanisms, on which superego formation rests, likewise advance from gross mechanisms of introjection of bad and good object images to selective internalization of such conceptualized standards regarding desirable human behavior. Only then can those processes of partial identification, to which the superego owes its existence, become sufficiently coordinated to integrate the different superego components into the psychic organization as a new functional structure.

During latency and adolescence the superego normally undergoes further maturation, which proceeds essentially along those very lines of building up a coherent system whose various functional components dovetail and collaborate with each other and also with the ego.

The core of the superego is certainly the law against patricide and matricide and the incest taboo; that superego fear continues and replaces castration fear can easily be observed in patients who unconsciously may still equate the superego with the threatening paternal—or their own—phallus. I mentioned this equation in the discussion of female superego development. But there is a tremendous step from the simple moral logic of castration fear, of fear of punishment and hope for reward, to the abstract moral level of a superego which has expanded from the taboo of incest and murder to a set of impersonal, ethical principles and regulations for human behavior. The superego can indeed mete out a wide range of experiences, from a general sense of responsibility to strong feelings of moral conviction and urgent obligation, from subtle pangs of conscience to overwhelming guilt feelings and remorse, from mildly self-virtuous feelings to profoundly rewarding moral self satisfaction.

This touches on the question whether we experience the existence of the superego only in case of conflict. I doubt whether this is so. Of course, we may forget our conscience. It may be silent. But to have "a good conscience," a feeling of moral self satisfaction, can involve intensely positive pleasurable experiences. Harmony between ego and ego ideal can produce a very enjoyable elated affective state. This relation between ego and superego is evidently not analogous to the relation between ego and id, whose existence we experience mainly in case of conflict. The reason for the difference is the survival of the child's relationship with his parents in the relationship between superego and ego. This also finds expression in the different qualities of castration fear and guilt feelings, to which I referred above. Castration fear has nothing to do with the child's love relations with his parents; but guilt feelings have their roots in the child's hostile and anxious as well as in his loving relationship with them. Clinically we know that persons whose superego has not developed under the influence of loving, kindly, guiding parents have castration and other infantile fears, but may be unable to experience real guilt feelings.

Whereas I have thus far done my best to stress the depersonified, abstract nature of the superego, my emphasis here is back again on the sort of personal relationship that we usually maintain, to some extent, with our conscience. Of course, the superego is deeply rooted in the unconscious; and we have no control over the powerful unconscious needs for punishment which determine so many unfortunate actions. But it is significant, from the functional point of view, that the mature autonomous superego has very definite preconscious and conscious representations in our ethical principles and ideals and in what we commonly call our conscience. They develop in the course of adolescence and will be discussed in this context.

In any case, we may say not only that the superego can deal with the self as with an object, but also the reverse: inasmuch as we can consciously experience the greater or lesser disparity between ego and ego ideal and are aware of

[128]

conflicts with our conscience, we can confront and effectively deal with them.

Considering these various aspects, we cannot doubt that the constitution of the superego, if successful, provides functions far more complex and valuable for the ego and the id than mere signal fears and simple self criticism. Reflecting the child's transition from his early dependent situation to a more active, independent position, it develops into a structure that has many facets and multiple functions. By coupling signal fears, self-critical and self-rewarding functions with guiding, inspiring, enforcing inner principles and demands, it can combine stop signals with positive directions to the ego. Moreover, it is a system that not only can activate the ego's defenses against specific, unacceptable instinctual strivings but also gain influence on the total ego by modifying its cathectic conditions and the discharge processes in general.

Thus, the superego must be regarded as a momentous, comprehensive structure formation developing in reaction to the child's oedipal and narcissistic strivings, to his forbidden sexual desires as well as to his destructive impulses. It represents a compromise in every direction. The oedipal conflict has been resolved, the ambivalence struggle has subsided, but their vestiges reappear and continue in the inner conflicts between ego and superego. The limitless narcissistic strivings of the child have been curbed and modified, but they survive in the ego ideal and in the ego's ceaseless efforts to measure up to its standards.

Tremendously increasing the endopsychic tensions, the superego develops into an autonomous central system for the regulation of the libidinal and aggressive cathexes of the self representations, independent of the outside world. It assumes an eminent part in the entire psychic economy. By gaining control of the course and modes of the discharge processes it exercises an enormous influence over our emotional and thought processes and our actions. However, the development of our concepts of value does not end with the establishment of a superego, even though our moral self evaluation remains predominantly a superego function.

The maturation of the ego and of critical judgment considerably modifies our concepts of value and our actions. Leading to an acceptance of what is realistic and reasonable, it accomplishes at least a partial victory of the reality principle, not only over the pleasure principle, but also over exaggerated "idealism" and thus over the superego. Only then do the superego functions work with more neutralized energy. In fact, the final maturation of both the ego and the superego sets in only after the tempest of instinctual conflicts during adolescence has subsided. Then we observe a gradual moderation of youthful idealism and illusions, leading to the setting up of more reasonable goals and to a further development of moral judgment: of the ability to test and to evaluate the outside and inside reality correctly, reasonably, and with greater moral tolerance, and to act according to such judgment.

Thus, whereas self perception always represents an ego function, the self evaluation of an adult person is not exclusively a superego function. Founded on subjective inner experience and on objective perception by the ego of the physical and mental self, it is partly or sometimes predominantly exercised by the superego, but is also partly a critical ego function whose maturation weakens the power of the superego over the ego.

Self esteem is the ideational, especially the emotional, expression of self evaluation and of the corresponding more or less neutralized libidinal and aggressive cathexis of the self representations.

These considerations lead to the conclusion that self esteem does not necessarily reflect the conflict between superego and ego. Broadly defined, the level of self esteem is expressive of the harmony or discrepancy between the self representations and the wishful concept of the self, which is by no means always identical with the unconscious and conscious ego ideal. Hence, disturbances of self esteem may originate from many sources and represent a very complex pathology: on the one hand, a pathology of the ego ideal or of the achievement standards and goals of the ego and, hence, of the self-critical ego and superego functions, and, on the other hand, a pathology of the ego functions and of the self representations. Increase or decrease of libidinal or aggressive discharge, inhibition or stimulation of ego functions, libidinal impoverishment or enrichment of the self caused by external or internal factors, from somatic, psychosomatic, or psychological sources, may reduce or enhance the libidinal or aggressive cathexis of the self representations and lead to fluctuations of self esteem. The influence of superego formation on the affective development discloses itself above all in the introduction of a new affective experience: the feeling of guilt. Comparatively independent of the outside world and probably the most insufferable of all unpleasurable experiences, guilt feelings are an affect signal which establishes an even more severe and certainly more universal and continual power over the ego than castration fear. Thus, they become the motive force of manifold new defensive devices. In general, the contribution of the superego to the organization and structuralization of emotional and ideational processes can hardly be overestimated.

Let me revert to my previous remarks concerning the proportions between libidinal, aggressive, and neutralized drive energy in the psychic organization, between the cathexes of the self and the objects with these different drives, and between the corresponding self- and object-directed drive discharges. I have emphasized the influence of these proportions on the discharge patterns and hence on all ego manifestations in the areas of feelings, thinking, and action.

Fundamentally, the superego appears to aim at an improved, more stable balance in these proportions. I stated that the narcissistic cathexes pilot all successful ego activities and, in turn, increase in their wake. In the course of superego formation, however, this mutual dependency between self esteem and object-directed ego expression undergoes significant changes. The superego is less concerned with external success or failure than with the degree of inner harmony or discordance between its moral codes and ego manifestations. On the one hand, it gains control over the general course of object-directed discharge processes. By curbing and modifying them, subject to inner moral standards, in a uniform way, irrespective of the specific object around which they are centered, these processes become far more resistant to dangerous external and internal instinctual influences.

This universal control effects, in turn, a central endopsychic regulation of the cathexis of the self representations and of self-directed discharge. Consequently, a more stable and enduring libidinal cathexis of the latter is established which cannot be as easily affected as before by experiences of rejection, frustration, failure, and the like. This cathectic stability normally finds expression in the maintenance of a sufficiently high average level of self esteem, with a limited margin for its vacillations, apt to withstand to some extent psychic or even physical injuries to the self. Thus the superego accomplishes, in general, a central regulation of the narcissistic and object cathexes and promotes the stability of both.

In summary, the superego introduces a safety device of the highest order, which protects the self from dangerous internal instinctual stimuli, from dangerous external stimuli, and hence from narcissistic harm.

Spiegel (1959) has shown how much the experience of inner coherence and continuity of the self depends on the gradual stabilization and sustenance of such a well-balanced cathectic situation.

I have stated that the centralized, regulating power of the superego can modify the course of the self- and object-directed discharge processes in a generalized way. But generalized modifications of all discharge patterns lend our thoughts, actions, and above all our feelings a characteristic color which finds expression in what we call our mood. Thus the superego also becomes a governing force for our moods and keeps them on a comparatively even level. This is why any pathology and deficiency of the superego functions will manifest itself in conspicuous disturbances of the mood level.

Inasmuch as the critical superego response does not remain limited to the disapproval or approval of specific impulses or actions but may morally condemn or praise the total self, the superego lowers or raises, indeed, the general level of self esteem. This affects all ego functions and influences our whole emotional state by creating mood vacillations. They are manifestations of processes which are definitely useful from the economic point of view. Since the superego is a guide for our self esteem and determines—albeit not exclusively—the rises and falls of the mood level, it may be properly called an indicator and regulator of the entire ego state, which serves a significant economic function. However, in this capacity the superego temporarily relinquishes its specific directive and enforcing functions in favor of an important but more primitive economic function. So long as guilt feelings refer to specific unacceptable strivings, they can advise us precisely what we should and should not do. But depressed or elated states have no such effect on the ego; they deal with the self in primitive terms of punishment and reward and are functionally at best of economic advantage to the ego.

Normally the two kinds of functions have their own place and supplement one another. Even in a person with a perfectly stable and effective superego, an intense superego pressure caused by moral failure may well spread out and induce a temporary state of depression. But in patients with a pathological archaic superego structure, we can observe that the superego is unable to do more than provoke self-punitive behavior or create recurring depressive mood deviations which do not inspire the ego to ward off and sublimate forbidden strivings. In this case, the constructive collaboration between self-critical and guiding faculties seems to be temporarily or permanently lost. Let us recall the type of patients who constantly act out impulsively and then pay for their sins with depressive conditions and the destructive results of their actions; persons whose superego is punitive but, in spite of this, never serves either as a moral preventive or as a moral incentive. Fundamentally, their moral conflict appears to survive and to remain unchanged from one depression and one impulsive action to the next.

In the course of the structural transformation and consolidation of the system during adolescence, the superego may temporarily function in such a manner for reasons which I shall have to discuss.

Let me conclude with a remark on the vicissitudes of self and object representations after final solution of the oedipus conflict. Superego formation and the beginning of latency signify the termination of the period of infantile repression, with consolidation and integration of all preoedipal and oedipal countercathectic formations into an organized unit. This result demonstrates, indeed, the remarkable influence which the processes of identification in the superego and ego exercise on the development of a coherent, consistent defense organization. But during this phase, the representations of the self and the object world also gain definite, lasting configurations. I pointed out above that the period of infantile repression succeeds in excluding a considerable sector of memories from the preconscious and conscious mind. Consequently, the object and self representations emerging with the subsiding of the infantile psychosexual conflicts bear the imprint of this exclusion as well as of the countercathectic ego formations which safeguard the results of infantile repression. The adolescent reactivation of early infantile conflicts again finds expression in the youngster's confusion about himself and the world and in the stormy vacillations of his self esteem, which we shall study in the final chapters.

9

Developmental Trends in the Latency Child and the Relations of Guilt to Shame and "Inferiority"[1] Conflicts

THE INFLUENCE of the moral system on the establishment of consolidated defenses and sublimated activities and the concomitant development of realistic ego goals gives the identification processes, during the period of latency, very specific guidance and direction. In conjunction with the further maturation of the ego and the object relations, these processes tremendously widen the scope of personal and social investments and of ego interests.

I have shown how, with the development of aim-inhibited physical, practical, intellectual, and emotional pursuits, the narcissistic cathexes, withdrawn from the erogenous body zones, spread out to representations of the entire body and mental self. These continuous cathectic redistributions and displacements to representations of all the executive organs and functions of the ego, and the correspondingly increasing multitude and variety of coordinated activities immensely fortify the child's experience of his self as a composite and

[1] I put the word "inferiority" in quotation marks because it belongs to the terminology of Alfred Adler and his followers. But it is my conscious intention to examine the meaning of this commonly used descriptive term from the standpoint of analytic ego psychology.

[136]

coherent identity. Moreover, the development of his identity feelings profits especially from the reinforcement of the sense of time rendered by the superego. This manifests itself in the firm establishment of the concepts of age, of future, and of future goals, which with the onset of latency finds great support, of course, from school. These concepts help to develop in the child a feeling of belonging to his age group, which facilitates the acceptance of his present position and identity as a child with a child's limitations, in contrast to that of an older child some grades above him or an adult into whom he will turn in the future.

In general, it helps children even to accept such individual differences from their peers which may emphasize their personal weaknesses. This brings the problem of group formation, and the feelings of group belonging and of group values into focus.

I have already stated that in the course of the oedipal period we can observe how, after the discovery of their sexual identities, the little boy and, more reluctantly, the little girl begin to develop a feeling of belonging to the members of the same sex. Entrance into school and the beginning of latency will, of course, reinforce this grouping and may soon carry it over from the distinction between the group of boys and the group of girls to other group differentiations—eventually to the point of discrimination between social, cultural, racial, national groups, and the like.

I have demonstrated how the male child's feeling of belonging to the group of males (despite its homosexual implications) normally strengthens his masculine position, while his "anti-girl" attitudes help—or rather compel—the little girl to accept, more or less resignedly, her feminine position. But the complications in her instinctual vicissitudes leave her for the most part in a more precarious balance, which finds expression in her vacillating feelings toward both "the girls" and "the boys." Secret or open admiration and wooing of boys may mingle in little girls with fearful, envious, aggressive attitudes toward them. Thus, until puberty, girls take much less pride in belonging to the group of girls. There are more variations and formations of different small cliques of either more feminine or more tomboyish or aggressively seductive little girls. The common persistence of such male group attitudes is certainly bound to keep alive the girl's earlier desire to join the ranks of the boys, to play with them, and eventually to conquer them by means of feminine seduction.

In any case, from the standpoint of superego and ego formation, it is significant that the experience of belonging to the same age and sex group not only reinforces the sense of personal identity but makes possible the development and acceptance of common group standards—ethical, social, physical, and intellectual. Some of these standards are based on peer relationships and are more or less in opposition to those of the adults; others derive from relationships to teachers and adult group leaders. This leads to a partial displacement of the child's relations and identifications from the parents onto such new authoritative figures; it is a process which becomes greatly intensified in adolescence. It reflects the limited autonomy of superego and ego in the latency child, who tends to reproject and reattach his superego, and likewise his ego goals, to dominant influential persons in the outside world. We here remember the different moral standards of children when they are with each other, from those effective in the presence of adults, especially parents and teachers. The establishment of group standards and group belongings assist the child further in testing his inner reality and in delimiting his present self and its position not only from the past but also from distant goals and the potential future position he may reach, if only he makes serious endeavors to live up to the demands of his external and internal guides.

While thus propelling the ego toward further structuralization and differentiation, the set of standards offered by the superego, if uniform and consistent, concomitantly stimulates the processes of organization to which I pointed previously.

In fact, we must realize that the growth and the increasing structuralization of the psychic apparatus constantly make new demands on the integrating, organizing forces which, I believe, are operative in all psychic structures, i.e., not only in the ego but also within the superego, where they guarantee the coherence and consistency of our scales of moral values and of the superego functions.

With the formation of the psychic systems, there arise difficulties in coping with the intersystemic as well as with the intrasystemic conflicts, to which Hartmann (1950) has called special attention. These intrasystemic conflicts may gain impetus with the increasing amount and variety of object investments and of different, possibly contradictory, identifications in the superego and the ego, which must be reconciled, combined, and organized, in order to allow for a coherent, goal-directed personality development that can promote normal identity formation and reinforce the feeling of inner continuity.[2]

The maturity and consistency of superego standards and ego goals, and the consistent influence of the moral system on

2 In this connection we recall Freud's remarks in *The Ego and the Id* (1923) on "the pathological outcome" if the ego's object identifications "become too numerous, unduly intense and incompatible with one another.... It may come to a disruption of the ego," Freud states, "in consequence of the individual identifications becoming cut off from one another by resistances" (p. 38).

the goals of the ego are, indeed, an indispensable prerequisite for the ego's ability to build up not only a coherent, effective defense structure but also a hierarchic organization of the different personal relations, ego identifications, ego interests, and ego functions. Since severely conflicting scales of values inevitably are reflected in dangerous discordances within the ego, superego and ego may indeed defeat each other's purposes by irreconcilable contradictions, which interfere with the development of superego and ego autonomy, with the ego's mastery of reality, its control of the id, and its adaptation to the object world.

I want to emphasize again that these processes of organization and reorganization within the psychic systems will not terminate before the end of adolescence. I believe that this is actually the core of Erikson's statement (1956) that the final identity "is superordinated to any single identification with individuals of the past" (p. 112). His formulations, unfortunately, do not clarify the continual and close interrelations between the infantile (and also the adolescent and postadolescent) processes of identification and the concomitant process of identity formation. His statement that identification as a mechanism is of limited usefulness (p. 112) is questionable, because identifications cannot be regarded as mechanisms and their usefulness for ego development is almost boundless. Combined with his further remarks (on the same page), his comments show a regrettable misunderstanding of these processes, of the vicissitudes of identifications, and their contribution to ego and superego formation and to the autonomy of these systems.

I hope my objections to Erikson's formulations will become clearer in the subsequent chapters dealing with the adolescent and postadolescent periods, when I shall focus once more on the superego and on these processes of organization to

[140]

which I am here referring. My brief clarification and the ensuing discussion bear reference to certain developmental problems, which have to be more carefully examined when we focus on adolescence. But the preceding clarification was necessary for the understanding of the conflicts which will be studied in this chapter, because they show up rather early in childhood.

Actually, some specific complications in the development of superego and ego can cause future identity problems. These can frequently be traced back to early preoedipal stages, when conflicting parental attitudes begin to exert their influences upon the weak infantile psychic organization. In the last chapter of this volume I shall give a few brief examples of such cases. Frequently, the disturbances arising from such contradictory attitudes become manifest when the child, on entering kindergarten and school, begins to build up rapidly broadening personal relations, and becomes subject to new educational, intellectual, social, ethical influences different from those of the home environment. I emphasized the fact that commonly superego and ego formation is supported and stimulated by the child's beginning contacts with a school world that now offers him new sublimations, new and different types of relations, and new identifications with teachers and with his peers. But children brought up in a confusing emotional and educational home atmosphere may at this time suddenly and painfully become aware of contradictions between the school world and the world at home, or within the family, with regard to sexual, human, social, ethical, and intellectual attitudes, goals, and standards. These experiences may throw them into a temporary state of lonesome confusion about right or wrong, good or bad, correct or incorrect, true or false, worthy or unworthy. Some of my adult patients with identity problems recalled, indeed, states

[141]

of loneliness in the beginning of latency, either at home or at school, or both. The earlier doubts concerning the parents' sexual identity, their conflicting attitudes and personalities, and their role in the family were then carried over to the sphere of values in general.

The history of such patients reveals that the internalization of such confusing parental attitudes at an early infantile stage may result in lasting contradictions in a person's unconscious and conscious sets of values; this not only may affect the establishment of stable personal relations with sufficient object constancy, and hence of consistent superego and ego identifications; it also predisposes the child to identity problems which may gain a dangerous momentum during adolescence and extend into the life of the adult.[3]

The early development of contradictory identifications, which predispose the child to identity problems, brings further into focus closely related aspects of ego and superego formation. Their discussion will serve as a preparation for the study of adolescent and postadolescent identity formation.

One issue, shame reactions and their relations to the guilt feelings, is a subject to which Erikson (1956) called particular attention in connection with the adolescent's self consciousness and his identity problems (p. 120, p. 142). Linked up with this are questions pertaining to the relations of the superego to guilt and shame, and of self esteem to the self feelings.

In view of the ubiquity of shame reactions and of their particular significance in persons with identity problems, Piers and Singer (1953) and Lynd (1958) were certainly jus-

[3] In this context one should also think about changes in the value system of a society. Different economic, ideological factors can have a confusing influence on the parental superego and the educational attitudes of the adult environment. The resulting contradictory scales of value are then handed down from the society to the child, via family, kindergarten, and school.

tified in criticizing the comparative neglect of the subject by psychoanalytic authors.

Hartmann and Loewenstein (1962) are of the opinion that shame can be distinguished from guilt only descriptively and not in terms of analytic psychology (p. 66). I am not in complete agreement with this view, though it is, of course, true that shame conflicts become part of superego conflicts. Nevertheless, the distinction between shame and guilt conflicts appears to be justified on clinical and theoretical grounds, because shame conflicts play a particular role in normal adolescent development; moreover, they make a regular, conspicuous appearance in patients with identity conflicts and, in such cases, are a characteristic expression of the patients' ego and superego pathology and their specific narcissistic conflicts. For this reason I have decided to discuss the nature of the shame and inferiority conflicts, and to examine the differences, the relation and the interplay between guilt, shame, and inferiority feelings from the theoretical and clinical point of view.

Of necessity, I must restrict my discussion of the shame reactions to the present frame of reference. Regarding their development, I may refer to my previous remarks in Part II and to Piers's and Singer's (1953) valuable book on this subject. Let us recall that shame arises rather early in reaction to pregenital (oral and especially anal) and to phallic-exhibitionistic strivings, and that it is reinforced in girls by their castration conflict. In this connection I want to stress again that the achievement of bowel control and of the discovery of sexual differences play a significant role in the development of the identity feelings.

Shame reactions are originally provoked when one's loss of instinctual control, physical defects (castration), and failures are exposed to others. Yet they normally become rather early manifestations of an internalized conflict.[4] Independent of exposure to others, they may thus commonly appear whenever we become aware of something disgraceful in ourselves. Comparing shame and guilt, Lynd (1958) maintains that shame, in contrast to guilt, always involves "the whole self." This statement is not quite valid, at least in so far as moral shame reactions, like guilt feelings, commonly bear reference to very specific strivings, and may spread out to the whole self only if they are intense.

It is, however, true that shame reactions have a much broader basis than guilt feelings and, because of their early infantile pregenital-narcissistic origins, may arise from many sources and conflicts, which involve all attributes of a person and not merely moral ones. In this respect it is significant that shame refers to visual exposure, guilt predominantly to verbal demands, prohibitions, and criticism. Their broad basis and the archaic type of anxieties which shame reactions may induce are certainly the reason why they can have such a self-annihilating overwhelming effect.[5] They may, for instance, develop in connection with moral problems as well as with questions of tact, manners, formal behavior, physical appearance; and, in a large number of people, in response to visible and more concrete external rather than personal and especially moral defects. Thus, people may feel ashamed not only of weaknesses such as deformities, of physical or mental

[4] A little boy of three was overheard by his mother, when he discovered that he had had an accident in bed. He expressed his inner shame conflict in the following monologue: "Oh! Oh! What happened? Terrible! I ought to be ashamed of myself! No! No! I won't! I will not be ashamed of myself!"

[5] Dr. Jay Shorr does not regard shame as a true reaction formation. He believes that certain feelings of shame may, because of the early infantile anxieties which they induce, give rise to reaction formations as a defense. Shorr's opinion deserves consideration.

illness, but also of low financial or social or racial status, and the like.

Of course, the tendency to shame reactions may become displaced to intellectual achievements. When we study such people, we detect, however, that their fears of exposure actually revolve not only around the thought content but essentially about the performance, the formal aspects of ideational expression which unconsciously is usually equated with anal production. These persons may thus undergo painful experiences of shame and humiliation mainly when their "formulations" are not equal to their perfectionistic expectations. Commonly we find in such persons profound guilt conflicts underneath or coupled with their shame conflicts. These guilt conflicts originate in the severe—mostly anal—aggressive cathexis of their thought processes which serve mainly competitive-narcissistic purposes.

This points to the differences between shame and inferiority conflicts. Though they are frequently coupled with shame reactions, feelings of inferiority do not arise as a reaction to specific instinctual strivings. Expressive of narcissistic defeat in any area of ego accomplishments, including the object relations, their infantile origins can frequently be traced back to all kinds of early narcissistic injuries and failures, i.e., to experiences preceding even the castration conflict. Thus, it would be wrong to say that inferiority conflicts are "based" on the castration conflict, although we know from our clinical experience that they inevitably mobilize unconscious castration and guilt conflicts.

In the *New Introductory Lectures* Freud (1932) refers to the erotic roots of the inferiority feelings. In his opinion, they originate in parental rejection and reflect, above all, conflicts between superego and ego. Thus Freud, while finding it difficult to distinguish inferiority from guilt feelings, suggests that we regard the first as the erotic supplement to the moral inferiority feelings. But this very suggestion underscores the differences.

I shall return to this issue. At this point I shall only state that feelings of both shame and inferiority manifest a person's conflicts with standards that regulate self esteem in terms of pride and superiority rather than moral behavior in relation to others. However, since shame arises as a reaction formation to forbidden instinctual strivings, it becomes at least partly integrated into the complex response of the ego to the superego. Feelings of moral shame will thus commonly appear in the mature adult whenever he becomes aware of low, mean, morally inferior impulses, that is, of infantile, especially pregenital, "degrading," contemptible strivings. Thus we may say that shame reactions range between guilt and inferiority feelings and may be coupled with either of them or both. The child who has accidents and cannot produce stools as expected feels (morally) bad, ashamed, and inferior.

With regard to the distinction of shame and inferiority feelings from guilt feelings, it is certainly of importance that guilt conflicts—as emphasized by Freud—seem to have a particular reference to hostility and harm to others, and in general to the quality of our object relations. In contrast, shame and likewise inferiority feelings and feelings of humiliation have much more elementary narcissistic-exhibitionistic implications. Inasmuch as such feelings develop from deficiencies or failures which betray weakness and deserve disgust and contempt, they refer essentially to the self as such only with regard to its power, its intactness, its appearance, and even its moral perfection but not in terms of our loving or hostile impulses and behavior toward others. It is interesting, indeed, that to some extent even moral pride and, the opposite, moral shame reactions have this conspicuously narcissistic quality, to which I have already referred in my discussion of shame and disgust in Chapter 6.

This is of paramount importance, since it explains the strange feeling of helplessness which so often accompanies shame reactions. In fact, quite in contrast to moral failures which we may overcome, many of those deficiencies which evoke shame and inferiority feelings cannot even be remedied: ugliness, physical defects, stupidity, incompetence, low social, racial, or economic status are often beyond repair. This is the reason why shame and inferiority feelings may secondarily arouse guilt feelings and be disguised by them. If an incompetent person fails in his work, he may be less willing to accept his irreparable inaptitude than to blame his inadequate efforts for his failures, because this leaves the door open for future improvements and success. But, of course, from our clinical experience we also know how often shame and inferiority feelings may conversely cover up or ward off guilt feelings. To return to the differences between shame and guilt, we can observe that not only in the area of sex and love but of personal relations in general the causes for shame and guilt may be diametrically opposed to each other. For instance, a person may feel guilty because of his sexual aggression but will be ashamed of impotence. He may feel guilty for having sadistically attacked and defeated or for having exploited another person, but he will be ashamed of being "a sucker," or of having suffered a "humiliating" defeat.

In general, sadistic impulses are apt to induce guilt, while masochistic, passive, dependent leanings, which may cause work inhibitions and hence ineptitude, tend to arouse feelings of shame and inferiority. For instance, a male patient, finding himself enslaved to an unworthy partner, experienced terrible feelings of shame and inferiority as long as he was unable to liberate himself; but as soon as he became aware of his sadistic impulses toward his wife and came close to the decision to desert her, he experienced intolerable guilt feelings. This is a typical example of the interplay between shame, inferiority feelings, and guilt reactions which we can constantly observe in our patients and also in normal persons.

This interplay frequently manifests itself in adolescent masturbation conflicts. A patient who in his adolescence suffered from compulsive masturbation would develop intense guilt feelings about his fantasies of "raping" a girl. He would regularly ward off such sadistic impulses by indulging instead in masturbation with passive, regressive fantasies of being spoiled and sexually gratified by beautiful girls who found great pleasure in taking the sexual initiative. However, this masturbation, which would rapidly lead to orgasm, would leave him with excruciating feelings of shame and inferiority, since he regarded his fantasies—correctly—as a manifestation of his passivity, his lack of masculinity, and impotence, i.e., of his castrated self image and his unconscious passive homosexual (oral and anal) wishes. These feelings would immediately result in new impulses to prove his masculinity by "raping" girls; inducing another outburst of guilt feelings, such impulses would have to be warded off once more by passive fantasies.[6]

Depending on the individual inner situation, the same provocative experiences may, of course, induce feelings of

[6] Later on this patient's passive strivings won out sufficiently to protect him from open aggressive and hence conscious guilt conflicts. What was left were obsessional traits and symptoms and depressive states accompanied by continuous, conscious shame and inferiority conflicts, with fears of exposure of his ineptitude in the realm of business and sex, fears of loss of money, and in particular fears of loss of financial and social status. After a considerable period of analytic work the hidden guilt conflicts could be brought to the surface and his superego pathology could successfully be approached.

shame mingled with guilt. To give a simplified example: when a man, in an outburst of rage, feels tempted to beat up his wife and children, he will feel guilty as well as ashamed of himself, the first, because of the severity of his anger, the second, because of his loss of control.

The differences, relations, and interplay between shame and guilt reactions immediately raise certain questions pertaining to ego ideal and superego, and their role in the development of guilt and shame. Piers and Singer (1953) and Lynd (1958) state that shame reactions arise whenever we cannot live up to our ego ideal. Regarding the ego ideal as an earlier structure, Piers thus separates it on a developmental level from the superego, which induces guilt feelings. In view of the fact, however, that shame can be caused, for instance, by sexual impotence, I believe that this separation is misleading, unless we broaden the concept of the ego ideal to a point where it loses its meaning. Since the ego ideal as a mature formation is so closely linked up with the moral demands and prohibitions of the superego and with its specific directive, enforcing, and self-critical functions, I believe, indeed, we do better to consider it, in accordance with Freud, as part of the superego system. I shall come back to this issue in the discussion of adolescence.

However, recalling the infantile forerunners of the ego ideal, which I discussed in Chapter 6, we can easily understand what Piers means. Inasmuch as the small child has not yet reached the stage of true idealization of his love objects and has not developed advanced notions of moral values, the infantile precursors of the ego ideal are still mainly the expression of pregenital drive regulations and of preoedipal and early oedipal (phallic) ambitions, i.e., of such values as physical strength and achievements, power, control over instinctual drives and objects, possessions and the like.

[149]

In Chapter 6 I described the advance of such primitive narcissistic goals and wishful self images, on the one hand, to the establishment of realistic, object-directed ego goals and, on the other hand, to the constitution of a mature ego ideal and of moral superego standards.

I stressed that with growing maturation of the ego these formations develop with the support of different and specific processes of identification: the first, from identification with realistic parental interests and parental attainment goals; and the second, from identification with idealized parental images and the internalization of moral parental demands, prohibitions, and criticisms. Since the ego ideal and our ethical standards arise from the infantile instinctual struggles, and are founded on the incest taboo and the law against patricide and matricide, they regulate in particular our sexual, personal, and social relations to the animate object world. Our ego goals, however, direct in particular our ego interests and serve our mastery of reality in general and our adaptation to it. I stressed that, with the development of the superego, they become subjected to its moral codes and, we may even say, interwoven with them. In the course of the oedipal period, ego achievements become indeed an expression of the child's willingness to displace his self- and object-directed instinctual strivings to aim-inhibited pursuits.

Nevertheless, we must realize that the child's ego identifications and ego formation follow a course that is directed by two masters: on the one hand, by parental moral and ethical standards or those of the superego respectively, and, on the other hand, by parental ego aspects and ego goals and by corresponding ego goals in the child, with limitations set by reality and the reality principle and by the ego's endowment and potentials. An effective surveillance of the ego by the superego and a smooth interplay and collaboration between superego standards and the goals and achievement standards of the ego will enable the child to combine the solution of his incestuous conflicts and the development of social behavior with the building up of ego functions, ego interests, and sublimations.

As we shall see, the instinctual upheaval during the adolescent period will again loosen the firm grip of the superego on the ego, and hence of the ego on the id. Under the influence of ego identifications with realistic parental images, and as a result of instinctual and ego maturation, the psychic systems are increasingly modified. This advancing modification will ultimately create a legitimate broad space for sexual and ambitious aims and strivings in the mature goals of the ego. However, whether the final re-establishment of a consistent superego control and of solid defenses in the ego succeeds, depends on the extent to which the adolescent struggle can be mastered. This will be studied in the final chapters of this volume.

Suffice it to emphasize once more that derivatives of early scales of value are kept alive in the ego goals even of the adult and in certain persons may play a very important part. To be sure, the values of physical, mental, intellectual perfection, of health and beauty, of sexual, vocational, and monetary success and power, of social, racial and national prestige rank high in our various modern societies. Such values and such elementary ambitions may easily collide with the moral and ethical codes which are set up by these same societies, are handed down to the parents and educators, and are internalized in the individual superego.

In fact, even if a person's social and vocational pursuits appear to be perfectly "reasonable" from the standpoint of his ego's potentials and of their potential future realization, they may still be the expression of excessively greedy and ambitious aggressive strivings for possessions and power, which may not be acceptable to his own conscience.[7]

Thus we may say that the goals of the ego are rather vulnerable. Even if seemingly object-directed and "rational," they may easily be employed in the service of primitive, aggressive-narcissistic strivings, unless they are kept under the firm surveillance of the superego.

These considerations are of great significance because they explain the ubiquity of adult shame and inferiority conflicts, and their interplay with guilt conflicts. Evidently, feelings of inferiority and shame, even of moral shame, preserve their reference to preoedipal and oedipal "premoral" notions of value. For this reason, they play a particular role during the adolescent period, which revives such early aims and strivings. Although they occur frequently even in normal adults, the prevalence of shame and inferiority over guilt conflicts after adolescence is mostly indicative of the type of narcissistic disturbances which cause identity problems. In the last chapter I shall return to this issue.

At this point I want to re-emphasize that feelings of moral shame, a reaction formation to pregenital strivings, may in adults develop in conjunction with guilt feelings. They are then indicative of superego conflicts. But feelings of shame maintain an even closer connection with the more primitive types of narcissistic conflicts, which induce feelings of inferiority and humiliation. These conflicts reflect the power of infantile libidinal and aggressive narcissistic strivings which may underlie a person's social, sexual, vocational, and intellectual pursuits.

These distinctions are of theoretical as much as of clinical

---

[7] We here recall that Alfred Adler, realizing the important role of such strivings in the psychology of some patients, built his theory of the neuroses exclusively on the "power drive."

significance, because they throw more light on the different mechanisms which regulate self esteem and on the way they may collaborate or work at cross-purposes with each other.

Strangely enough, since the time when Freud relinquished the idea of "ego drives" and introduced the structural concepts, we have been more concerned with the self-critical functions of the superego, which passes moral judgment, than with those of the ego, whose evaluation of the self covers a much broader field.

What we learned from our comparative study was, first of all, that the superego, judging in moral terms of right or wrong, good or bad, chiefly regulates our personal and social relations and behavior, and even evaluates our ego pursuits essentially from this perspective. Furthermore, the mature self-critical ego, though participating in this moral self evaluation, also judges our ego functions and our practical relations to reality, including those to the inanimate object world. Finally, the self-critical ego evaluates behavior not only in terms of correct or incorrect, true or false, appropriate or inappropriate, reasonable or unreasonable, but also from the standpoint of utilitarian and ambitious "worldly" ego goals ("self interests") with regard to their effectiveness, and success.

Unfortunately, the ultimate collaboration between self-critical superego and ego functions is often not smooth enough to prevent clashes between the moral codes of the superego and these utilitarian-ambitious goals of the ego. Success achieved with the aid of powerful aggressive-narcissistic strivings may raise a person's self esteem by inducing feelings of pride and superiority, while it may be unconsciously, or even consciously, profoundly condemned by his conscience. To give an extremely commonplace practical example: a highly successful, brilliant but ruthless career,

[153]

leading to great achievements, to a position of power and the acquisition of wealth and of high social status, may well induce severe moral conflicts, which may ultimately ruin the career.

On the other hand, high moral achievements, which are unfavorable and opposed to the "power" goals of the ego, may not infrequently be regarded as signs of weakness by the self-critical eye of the ego. A person, for instance, who sacrifices his career to his strict ethical principles may be inclined to despise himself for his lack of aggressiveness. However, such a description of potential collisions between moral (superego and ego) standards and the ambitious goals of the ego simplifies matters considerably, since regressive processes in either system may lead to clashes between conscious and unconscious goals and standards and corresponding self-critical functions.

It may be advisable to describe such particular complications from the structural point of view. To begin with, the lowering of moral self esteem, which evokes guilt or moral shame is caused by conflicts between ego and superego and reflects disharmony between (conscious or unconscious) ego-ideal components and the self representations. However, I have also spoken of the dangers inherent in contradictions within the superego and the ego ideal. Since even normally our conscious ideals may differ from those deeply ingrained in our unconscious, a person's conscious moral self evaluation may approve of actions which are severely condemned and punished by unconscious infantile superego components. As I already asserted, the conscious and unconscious narcissistic conflicts arising in the ego that lead to loss of self esteem cover an even wider area. Such conflicts develop from discordance between wishful self images which embody the narcissistic goals of the ego and a self that appears to be fail-

[154]

ing, defective, inferior, weak, contemptible in comparison. These narcissistic conflicts are apt to evoke feelings of inferiority and shame. As long as the conscious and unconscious self-critical ego functions evaluate the ego's attitudes, pursuits, and activities from the viewpoint of consistent, mature ego goals and as long as they operate in close touch with the superego and with reality, they are a most useful instrument of the ego.

However, there may be all sorts of complications caused by conflicts, on the one hand, between contradictory, conscious or preconscious, goals of the ego and, on the other hand, between reasonable and realistic ego goals and the potential multitude of more or less primitive, unconscious instinctual-narcissistic aims. Only under the regulating influence of a stable superego will the ego be able to cope with such discordances.

In the final chapter we shall study how in case of immaturity of the psychic systems or of a fragility of their structure, causing serious regressive processes, dangerous intrusions of infantile narcissistic and instinctual aims into the codes of the superego and the goals of the ego may occur. They may bring about a disintegration of object relations and identifications, and hence of ego and superego functions, leading to experiences of object loss and "loss of the self," and, possibly, to psychotic manifestations.

Part III

Puberty and the Period of Adolescence

10

Puberty Changes and Their Influence on the Experience of Identity and the Relations to the Other Sex

IN HER RECENT paper on "Adolescence" Anna Freud (1958) tried to explain why, in the opinion of all analytic experts in this field, our insight into the confusing emotional manifestations and symptomatology of this developmental period is as yet far from complete. She pointed out that adolescents are usually resistant to analysis, and adult patients, though producing sufficient adolescent memory material, usually do not revive the corresponding adolescent emotional reactions. It is my impression that in the analysis of adults we may, in addition, tend to be more concerned with the reconstruction of their infantile history than with the full exploration of their adolescent development. Focusing on this stage, we frequently discover that this was the time when the patient's neurosis took on a characteristic configuration. It is certainly true that adult patients rarely revive their adolescent emotional reactions; but even in this respect we may find exceptions. Patients who suffer from protracted adolescent problems may still, at the age of thirty or so, show the adolescent fluidity in their moods and in the current symptom formation, with clinical manifestations changing from neurotic to delinquent, perverse, or borderline psychotic.

[159]

In the context of this discussion, Anna Freud compared the adolescent's resistances to analytic treatment with the difficulties encountered in patients during periods of mourning or during unhappy love affairs; and she emphasized how much the emotional situation of the adolescent has in common with these two states.

Berta Bornstein and Nathan Root (1957) had already called attention to the significant role of mourning in the struggle of the adolescent, who must disengage himself from his parents and embark on a search for new objects.

But why does the adolescent pass through such violent and peculiar affective crises? Why does he show such a tendency to rapid, sudden swings of mood? What are the nature and origin of these moods? And for what reasons do so many adolescents suffer from recurring painful states of depression and despair, which may involve not only severe guilt conflicts but harassing feelings of shame and self consciousness to the point of hypochondriacal body preoccupations or paranoid fears?

Moreover, why do we find embedded in the adolescent's conspicuous and unique emotional manifestations such characteristic, disturbing fluctuations in his feelings for others and in his self feelings, his feelings of identity? Why does he at one time show a close relatedness to the world, to people, to nature or art or God, in conjunction with rich experiences of "I am I, I live, and the world is mine and will be mine," while at other times he has painful doubts about the meaning of life and the world, about himself and his role in the world, or even suffers from desperate feelings of isolation and loneliness and is convinced of the nothingness of his existence, of life, of his own life and future?

In the preceding chapter I laid the ground for a study of the psychic processes causing these turbulent emotional phenomena. But before we embark on it, we must visualize the inner situation of the adolescent, which Anna Freud (1936, 1958) and Helene Deutsch (1944), among other authors, have so beautifully described.

In point of fact, adolescence is life between a saddening farewell to childhood—i.e., to the self and the objects of the past—and a gradual, anxious-hopeful passing over many barriers through the gates which permit entrance to the as yet unknown country of adulthood. Beginning with his infantile love objects, the adolescent not only must free himself from his attachments to persons who were all-important during childhood; he must also renounce his former pleasures and pursuits more rapidly than at any former developmental stage. Preparing himself to leave home sooner or later, he must reach out for adult sex, love and responsibility, for personal and social relations of a new and different type, for new interests and sublimations, and for new values, standards, and goals which can offer him directions for his future life as an adult.

This necessitates a complete reorientation, leading to structural and energic transformations, to economic-cathectic redistributions, and to a drastic overhauling of the entire psychic organization.

I do not intend to deal with all the aspects of these processes. What I shall mainly discuss is the remodeling of the adolescent's ego and superego, and its interrelationship with the development of his identity feelings, his object relations, and his identifications, whose vicissitudes find a reflection in the states of his mood.

In his paper on identity, Erikson (1956) deals with adolescent object relations in a rather casual manner, in terms of " 'Intimacy vs. Isolation' [as] the core conflict which follows that of 'Identity vs. Identity Diffusion' " (p. 124). But the adolescent's development of intimacy with others—with his peers, his elders, the opposite sex—is a very complex and conflict-ridden process that follows as well as interacts with identity conflicts and produces such problems. Again, I cannot help feeling that somehow Erikson disconnects identity from identifications, and both from object relations, and object relations from those conflicts around which the emotional turmoil and the disturbances of this stage are centered. These conflicts are aroused by the psychobiological changes in the adolescent, who feels himself in the grip of overwhelming instinctual impulses, which he must soon learn to master, since before long he will have to make the most important decisions of his life: vocational choice, which will determine his work and his future economic and social situation, and the choice of a love object—ultimately of a marital partner.

Thus, I should like first to emphasize some turning points in the adolescent's instinctual development and in the establishment of relations with the opposite sex. Of course, I cannot go into the complexities of the instinctual conflicts aroused by the onset of puberty. Let it suffice, first of all, to point to the significant influence of the anatomical and physiological puberty changes on the child's identity feelings and on identity formation.

The most incisive and upsetting experiences are the boy's first ejaculations and the onset of menstruation in the girl. We are familiar with the child's ambivalent reactions to these major events. Since the boy's first ejaculations commonly lead him to masturbation, they revive his castration fears and evoke guilt conflicts of such intensity that frequently the pleasure of becoming a man is overshadowed or smothered by long-lasting fears of this step. The beginning of menstruation in the girl arouses different but potentially even more dangerous conflicts, since genital bleeding is bound to reanimate the infantile belief in her castration. In spite of their well-known negative and anxious responses to this event, however, we can observe that, nowadays, girls commonly display much more pride in getting their periods than do boys with regard to their ejaculations and wet dreams. Of course, many girls refuse to accept the monthly bleeding: they hate it, try to deny and to hide it, and carry on strenuous physical activities during menstruation. But many girls openly brag about their menses to each other and even to adults, whereas boys frantically try to hide the physiological manifestations of puberty from adults and discuss them only secretly with each other; this is simply because, in contrast to menstruation, their ejaculations are usually accompanied by orgastic experiences and may lead to masturbation and not rarely to transitory homosexual play until heterosexual activity can assert itself.

Although adult women are often sexually more excitable during their menstrual periods than at other times, menstrual pain, discomfort, and fear of touching the bleeding genitals commonly prevent the young girl from masturbating, at least during the period. In adolescent girls, therefore, we rarely find *conscious* masturbation conflicts of such severity as in boys. The punitive aspects of their monthly bleedings tend in any event to absorb their guilt feelings. In fact, we know that the onset of menstruation frequently brings about a rather rapid, visible swing from the tomboy role to the assumption of a masochistically colored feminine position. Sometimes this decisive step is preceded by vacillations between a provocatively boyish and a somewhat forced feminine behavior during prepuberty, with concomitant sexual identity conflicts. Subsequently, the experience of menstruation, in conjunction with the general body changes, may fortify the feelings of feminine identity already in the beginning

[163]

of puberty, whereas the boy's masculine position and his feelings of sexual identity are not necessarily strengthened at the beginning of his new, guilt-evoking sexual experiences.

At any rate, in both sexes the anxious and ambivalent reactions to the physiological manifestations of puberty cause cathectic displacements to the conspicuous bodily, mental, and intellectual changes, which are the result of the adolescent maturation processes. As we shall see, these changes exert a significant influence on the modification of ego and superego in adolescence and hence on the identity feelings and identity formation.

If the boy feels guilty and is ashamed of his ejaculations, he certainly takes all the more pride in the sometimes remarkably sudden growth of his body and his penis. He looks eagerly to the appearance of his secondary sexual characteristics, of pubic hair, a mustache, and the change of voice, which commonly develop some years after the beginning of ejaculations. But, significantly, when these changes do come about, they may again provoke shame rather than unmingled feelings of pride. In girls, too, the pride in the growth of their breasts, their axillary and pubic hair, and in the development of feminine curves, is for years frequently mingled with feelings of shame. Apparently, such feelings are particularly aroused by the girl's "nipple erotism" whose significance Sarlin (1963) recently stressed again. In addition, the appearance of acne, which so often haunts adolescents of both sexes, may reinforce the propensity for shame reactions. Again, such shame reactions may cover up guilt conflicts, because the skin eruptions may be regarded as a result of masturbation.

The striking changes in the general appearance may, within a few years, transform rough, sloppy, awkward boys into strong and sleek young men, and "ugly little duckling" girls—almost overnight—into attractive, poised and charming young women. But in conjunction with the physiological signs of sexual maturation these continuous body changes will, alternately and in waves, either confuse or confirm the adolescent's identity feelings. They will be slowly accepted to the extent to which the instinctual and narcissistic problems of adolescence find a solution.

This leads us to the relations between the sexes. You may recall my remarks on the "anti-girls" attitudes of boys during the latency years, attitudes which may become even more pronounced during prepuberty. They are demonstrated very nicely by the example of a boy named Kenneth. In prepuberty he founded an "Anti-Girls-Club" of boys, who, abandoning the company of girls, were busy inventing practical jokes which would annoy and frighten them. When a club member was observed consorting with a girl, he was punished or contemptuously expelled from the club. It was characteristic of Kenneth during this period that he completely rejected his younger sister, who loved, admired, and constantly wooed her brother without any success. Not until Kenneth, after leaving home in his late adolescence, fell in love with a girl, did he begin gradually to accept his sister and to develop a good relationship with her. However, the poor rejected girl now had a difficult time overcoming her inhibitions and her masochistic attitudes toward boys.

Although Kenneth's puberty and adolescence did present unusual problems, the transition, especially in boys, from the aggressiveness or comparative indifference toward the opposite sex during latency and prepuberty, to the time of beginning erotic interest in the other sex is always difficult. The entire adolescent period abounds with sexual and ambivalence conflicts, with anxieties and narcissistic struggles, which find expression in the youngster's sexual and aggressive

[165]

acting out and in his vacillating behavior toward his own and the opposite sex. I shall say more about these difficulties in the discussion of the superego and its modification during adolescence. At the moment I only wish to point to the conspicuous differences in the sexual behavior and sexual acting out of adolescent boys and girls.

I made references above to the frequency of homosexual play in boys. In girls, masturbatory fantasies and latent homosexual "crushes" are more common than masturbation and homosexual activity, up to the time when psychosexual relations between boys and girls set in. At this stage, the dangers, such as illegitimate pregnancy, promiscuity, and venereal disease, may be promptly warded off by escape into regressive, incestuous fantasies. With regard to the incestuous wishes, we again find more acting out in boys than in girls. Whereas female patients usually recall fleeting incestuous fantasies and dreams during adolescence, several of my male patients attempted as adolescents to seduce their younger or older sisters by exhibiting their penises. It is of interest that in all these cases the sisters ignored the seduction; but some of them responded to the brother's advances by immediately making ostentatious phone calls to boy friends. From such and similar observations one may infer that many adolescent boys tend to protect themselves from the threat of real heterosexual relations by regressive flight into such more or less infantile forms of incestuous behavior, while girls conversely may ward off these incestuous temptations by escaping into flirtations and conquests of other boys. In such relations, they commonly feel better protected than the boys by their fears of defloration, pregnancy, and waywardness. In general, the revival of their infantile castration conflicts by the onset of menstruation and the frequent withdrawal of narcissistic cathexis from the genitals, originally caused by this conflict, fortify the girls' sexual defenses, but there is a more rapid advance of their emotional relations to the other sex than is common in boys. Their feminine position, which forbids direct, aggressive sexual approaches, further reinforces their instinctual control. Thus it is usually the girl who sets definite limits to the boy's sexual aggression. This eventually compels many adolescent boys of middle-class society to shift the field of sexual experimentation—more or less unwillingly —to prostitutes or to girls who are easily available and assume this role. Full sexual relations with girls of the same social strata develop in a certain segment of the population only toward the end of adolescence. Up to that time the relations between girls and boys usually remain limited to "necking" and "petting" activities, and in either sex the emotional as well as physical relations serve narcissistic aims of aggressive sexual and emotional self assertion more than the attainment of full genital pleasure and the development of deeper love relations between the sexes. As we shall see, this prolonged phase of increased narcissism plays a significant part in the building up of the ego and the remodeling of the superego during adolescence.

I have already asserted that girls commonly are known to mature emotionally more rapidly than boys. I have also made mention of the frequently rapid swing to the feminine position in puberty. Subsequently, girls often make a rather quick emotional transition from the incestuous to exogamous love objects. Eager to establish emotional rather than sexual rapport with boys in early adolescence, they may feel ready to marry and have children at the age of eighteen. But if they marry early, they may choose parental (or older brother) figures more frequently than do boys. Sometimes the more rapid advance of psychosexual maturation in girls may be due to greater inhibitions or limitations regarding their in-

[167]

tellectual interests and vocational choices. But the most significant factor may be the girl's tremendous need for narcissistic supplies from men, a need caused by the narcissistic injuries of the past. Moreover, the tempestuousness of the wish for a child, which gains momentum from the past castration conflict, combines with the stronger prohibitions and fears regarding extramarital sexual relations to propel girls toward early marriage. Marriage appears all the more desirable since it promises security—emotional and material. Contrary considerations cause the adolescent boy to shy away from the idea of an early marriage, whose financial burdens would rest mainly on his shoulders, possibly at the expense of his postadolescent vocational, intellectual, and cultural development and his career. Predominantly for this reason, marriages contracted before the end of adolescence are generally not too durable. In most such cases it is the young husbands who complain about having committed themselves too early to marital responsibilities, and who want to escape from them.

This concludes my very sketchy remarks on those sexual experiences and events in adolescence which are pertinent to the problems under discussion. What the adolescent's instinctual development demonstrates so very impressively is the point to which I wished to call special attention. It shows how, in climbing up the tortuous ladder to adulthood, he seems to experience at every new step anxiety, confusion, disorganization, and a return to infantile positions, followed by propulsion and reorganization at more advanced and more adult levels.

Such processes, to be sure, can be observed at any developmental stage. But during the dramatic adolescent period we see what Helene Deutsch (1944) described as a "clash" between progressive and regressive forces. This clash leads to a far-reaching temporary dissolution of old structures and organizations, in conjunction with new structure formations and the establishment of new hierarchic orders, in which earlier psychic formations definitely assume a subordinate role, while new ones acquire and sustain dominance.

The adolescent's propensity to recurring swift temporary regressions in all areas and systems obviously results from the all-too-powerful assault of instinctual forces on his ego. Being itself engaged in continuous growth and change, the ego is certainly bound to reinstate past positions before it can cope with the formidable task of finding new ways of instinctual control and new avenues of discharge that will help the adolescent not only to relinquish his childhood attachments but also to gain the optimal and socially permissible degree of instinctual and emotional freedom needed for the building of adult sexual and personal relationships.

11

The Instinctual and Emotional Conflicts of the Adolescent and the Remodeling and Growth of His Psychic Structures

W‌E KNOW THAT during the adolescent struggle the defenses established during latency become so badly battered that they may partly break down under the onslaught of instinctual impulses. How does the adolescent manage to reconstitute, reorganize, and resolidify his defense system?

At this point, it may be helpful to compare the situation in adolescence with the childhood period of the passing of the Oedipus conflicts. The oedipal child has to repress his sexual and hostile impulses in favor of affectionate attachments to his parents. In adolescence, the sexual maturation process leads to a temporary revival of preoedipal and oedipal instinctual strivings, thus reviving the infantile struggle. But now the incestuous sexual and hostile wishes must be finally relinquished. Moreover, the adolescent's affectionate ties to the parents must also be sufficiently loosened to guarantee his future freedom of object choice and to permit him a sound reorientation toward his own generation and a normal adjustment to adult social reality. This is the cause of his grief reactions, which have no parallel in childhood. What makes this emotional task even harder is the fact that it involves, in addition, a definite and final abandonment of his practical and emotional dependency on the parents. Freud (1905) regarded this detachment from parental authority as one of the most significant, but also one of the most painful, psychic achievements.

In fact, the adolescent will soon "come of age" and thereby reach a point of no return, indicating that society regards him as capable of being his own master. Even though his practical dependency may extend to the twenties, or longer, this step signifies that the last phase in the solution of the oedipal conflicts must also bring about a final liberation from the symbiotic bonds with the family. His liberation is necessary for the ultimate establishment of the autonomy and independence of ego and superego, and is characteristic of this most significant period of identity formation. The adolescent's struggle may be complicated further by discrepancies in the concomitant, rapid growth of the ego, which is not always commensurate with the advance of instinctual development. I shall return to this problem below.

Superego formation assists the child in the solution of his oedipal and ambivalence conflicts and enables him to achieve a certain independence of external social and cultural influences even at that early stage. In the adolescent no new psychic system arises from his efforts to break away from his infantile love objects. However, his struggles for maturity and final liberation from his family bonds certainly find support from remarkable modifications and new structure formations developing in his superego and ego.

Of course, we know that during adolescence the superego becomes readjusted and consolidated, but what precisely does this process of consolidation involve? The necessity for a resetting of the defense system has already been mentioned. However, such reorganization of the defenses certainly presupposes and depends upon a far-reaching remodeling of the superego system. Since the superego is built up by virtue of partial identifications with idealized parental images, with parental standards, demands, and prohibitions, this question leads directly back to the problem of identifications.

I have pointed out that inasmuch as identifications acquire defensive functions, they enable the child to tolerate and accept instinctual frustrations, emotional deprivation, or even object loss, and that they arise, at least partly, in reaction to such experiences. Thus, we might easily infer that the adolescent, who now must definitely give up his oedipal love objects, would achieve this mainly by means of even stronger identification with them in his superego. But what actually happens is much more complicated, for good reasons.

At this point we must recall that identifications originate in the enduring psychobiological dependency of the child on his parents and that his infantile ego formation rests upon these identifications. "The weaker the child's ego," says Helene Deutsch (1944), "the more it resorts to identification with adults in its adjustment to the adult world" (p. 7). But up to his adolescence, even the child with normal ego strength learns to adapt himself to society—and to reality in general—less by direct and immediate contact than through the medium of his close relations and his identifications with his parents and parental figures. To the extent to which his ego has matured and established its secondary autonomy and independence, however, these identifications must lose an essential part of their function. Thus, contradictions must arise between the adolescent's need to cope with the loss of his infantile love objects by fortifying his identifications with them, and the fact that these very identifications become more and more dispensable.

With regard to the superego we must realize that, in comparison with the situation during the oedipal stage, its goals

[172]

and functions must undergo remarkable changes, at least as far as sex is concerned. During the infantile period of super-ego formation, the child commonly resolves his oedipal con-flicts with the aid of defenses which enable him to repress and inhibit his forbidden instinctual impulses to the point of more or less renouncing sexual activities in general. In adolescence the superego must once more enforce the incest taboo, yet at the same time it must open the barriers of repression and lift the burden of countercathexes—it must do so sufficiently to guide the adolescent on his road to the sexual freedom of the adult and to mature personal and love relationships. These contradictory aims are reflected in the vicissitudes and reorganization of his object relations and identifications, and hence in the changes which superego, ego, and id undergo in the course of adolescence. Before examin-ing these, however, I must first underline certain reservations with regard to my preceding statements.

When we observe that the adolescent's identifications with his parents lose some of their significance, or when we speak of his grief over loss of the incestuous love objects, we must immediately add that the final breaking of the oedipal ties, the establishment of new object relations, and the processes of new structure formation and reorganization during ado-lescence are successful only as long as they do not deplete the libidinal investments or eradicate the identifications of the past. They merely reduce them and displace them onto new objects, change their qualities, and subordinate them to new attachments and partly to new identifications (A. Katan, 1937). Approaching this problem from the structural point of view: the superego cannot be remodeled, reorgan-ized, and consolidated, and new personal and sexual relations, new ego structures and ego functions cannot be built up and integrated unless these new formations are allowed to grow

[173]

organically from those of the past. As a matter of fact, in adults the survival of unambivalent relations and of certain fundamental identifications with their parents can almost be used as evidence that in their adolescence these individuals had succeeded in renouncing their infantile desires and in breaking their symbiotic ties with the family.

In the paper I alluded to previously, in which Anna Freud (1958) describes the various devices employed by the adolescent in his endeavors to break his ties to the family, she also points to the serious implications of an "inner loss" of his infantile love objects at this stage.

In Chapter 12 I shall briefly discuss the severe pathology which develops when the adolescent permanently withdraws cathexis from his infantile love objects because he cannot otherwise master his excessively powerful ambivalence conflict with them. Here I merely want to stress that in this case there may occur processes of persistent or even irreversible profound regression in all systems. These processes resist the adolescent's frantic efforts to replace the infantile love objects with new persons, and to build up relations and reactive types of identifications with the latter. Subsequently, the adolescent's development may be arrested. Superego as well as ego functions may disintegrate and serious and confusing symptomatology may develop. Should the clinical picture be suggestive of a psychosis, it may present differential-diagnostic difficulties: in youngsters constitutionally and ontogenetically predisposed to psychosis, the psychophysiological instability of this period and the adolescent proclivity to recurrent deep regressions are, indeed, apt to set truly psychotic processes in motion.

At any event, in such grossly disturbed adolescents we may find profound subjective and objective identity problems, which far transcend the limits of what can commonly be

[174]

observed in adolescence. However, it is significant that even within the margin of normal development adolescents may pass through transient periods of narcissistic retreat to the point of real "inner" object loss and loss of identity. What is decisive is less the brief duration than the reversibility of such states. Normally they are followed by a return to the object world and by renewed progression.

Focusing now on the specific vicissitudes of the ego and superego identifications of the adolescent, we realize, first of all, that probably the most incisive and difficult step is the gradual establishment of enduring new identifications with the parents as sexually active persons, who will ultimately grant him, too, the right to engage in sexual and other adult activities.

It is not surprising that these identifications, which were unacceptable in the past, can become fully ego syntonic and attain dominance only to the extent to which superego and ego become reconstructed and consolidated, and reach a new level of strength, autonomy, and maturity. In fact, these identifications, which open the gates to adult sexual freedom, only gradually become an integral part of the adolescent's ever-widening identifications with the grownups in all areas of the ego which develop under the influence of new or modified superego identifications. This leads to the changes which the moral codes of the superego must undergo in the course of adolescence.

Simplifying matters considerably, I would briefly define these changes as follows. Whereas in childhood the voice of the superego stated: "If you identify with the parental moral standards, demands, and prohibitions, you will be granted sexual pleasure in the adult future," it must now convey: "You are permitted to enjoy adult sexual and emotional freedom and freedom of thoughts and actions to the

[175]

extent to which you renounce your infantile instinctual desires, loosen your childhood attachments, and accept adult ethical standards and responsibilities."

The adolescent is thus confronted with the complex and confusing task of toning down the idealized sexually prohibitive parental images, of reconciling them with realistic concepts of sexually active and increasingly permissive parents, and at the same time of building up new sets of moral and ethical standards based on a firm re-establishment of the incest taboo. We realize that this presupposes significant changes in the content and qualities of the ego ideal and superego—changes which are not merely the result of identification processes but which, as I will show further on, eventually gain strong reinforcement from new structure formations in the maturing and increasingly autonomous ego.

In the preceding discussion of superego formation in Part II of this volume, I have already stressed that contradictions in the parental attitudes and standards, or between the educational atmosphere at home and at school, may interfere with the establishment of consistent superego and ego identifications and create early identity problems, which may acquire dangerous momentum during adolescence. These dangers are connected with the changes which the superego must undergo during this period. Since the processes which bring about these transformations involve a reconciliation and integration of the most opposing goals and aims and of very contradictory identifications, they must temporarily weaken both the superego and the ego even in the normal adolescent whose psychic structures rest on a solid basis. The failure to resolve these contradictions becomes evident in many of our patients, whose absurd concepts of becoming adult may range from the fantasy that growing up means the attainment of complete instinctual freedom to the idea that it means complete instinctual renunciation. Thus it is no wonder that for a shorter or longer period these processes of transformation will cause marked fluctuations in the adolescent's superego functions and in his behavior, and disturb not only his relations to his parents but his object relations in general. Struggling for a partial lifting of his repressions, the adolescent will suffer from severe sexual, narcissistic, and ambivalence conflicts, which will become manifest in his attitudes toward persons of both sexes. During this struggle, to which I referred in Chapter 10, his ego will experience increased id and superego pressures and may alternately yield to or actively rebel against the superego and, overthrowing it, join forces with the id. More or less stormy periods of sexual and aggressive acting out and of narcissistic inflation thus may alternate with periods of repentance, of ascetic ideals, of strictly abstinent, moral behavior, and often of guilt, shame, and inferiority feelings.

From this acting out we indeed gain the impression that the psychophysiological sexual development, which is accompanied by rapid and visible body changes and concomitant mental growth of the ego, creates tremendous amounts of surplus psychic energy. This energy tends to feed and liberate not only the sexual and hostile impulses but also the unlimited narcissistic strivings that had once been absorbed by the constitution of superego identifications. In fact, to the extent to which he removes himself from his infantile love objects, the adolescent passes through a prolonged stage of overinvolvement with narcissistic aims and preoccupations *at the temporary cost* of truly object-directed goals. Anna Freud (1936) and Helene Deutsch (1944) have both commented on this intensification of narcissism in adolescence. As we shall see, however, in normal development, this ultimately gains a significant territory for the ego and the object relations.

What lends special coloring to the adolescent's vacillations and acting out is the drastic resetting of the defenses caused by the necessity to control and check the increased demands of the instinctual forces. It would be interesting to study precisely what changes the defense organization undergoes in these circumstances. But this problem is only peripheral to my topic and would lead too far afield.

Suffice it here to mention the regressive features in the defensive operations caused by the transitory, partial collapse of the superego and the repressive barriers. Trying to ward off his overpowering instinctual strivings, the adolescent may again call upon primitive defenses, such as denial, and upon infantile introjection and projection mechanisms. Or he may attempt to ward off sexual drives with aggression, or to escape from genital to pregenital, from masculine-aggressive to passive-feminine goals, from heterosexual to narcissistic-homosexual attachments and activities, and back again; from objects of his age to older persons, or even to incestuous objects, and the reverse. For this reason the adolescent may develop some forms of behavior that might suggest psychopathy or even psychosis.

In his struggle for a reconciliation between the opposing goals of the superego and the id, the adolescent may find aid from persons outside the family (or also from social, political or religious groups), who at this phase lend themselves better than the parents to repersonifications and reprojections of both superego and id. Pure and saintly, or seductive and ruthless men or women may thus alternately be admired and emulated or despised and hated, because they represent the adolescent's own sexual temptations and ambitions, or the virtue, humility, and chastity he seeks. But this is not all.

When we observe the types of persons whom adolescents glorify, revere, and emulate, or only imitate for briefer or longer periods, we also realize that the endeavors to remodel the ego ideal and superego lead to an intense revival of infantile superego precursors and of values expressive of pregenital and phallic-narcissistic selfish pleasure and power aims rather than moral goals. In fact, the adolescent's heroes or heroines may catch his eye because of their physical strength or attractiveness, or because of their sexual successes or their social glamour, wealth, ruthless career, and prominence in the fields of sport or art or science, of business or finance or politics, or even of crime. Not rarely the adolescent does indeed glorify prostitutes or gangsters and sometimes, unfortunately, join their ranks.[1] Moreover, his admiration for such persons and groups, or for the values they represent, may find expression in transient but intense homosexual or heterosexual "crushes," which frequently have a rather sadomasochistic coloring.

These phenomena reveal that the relationship between superego and ego may become temporarily deinstinctualized and repersonified and that the ego ideal may be partly replaced with pseudo-idealized, glamorous, wishful self and object images, which may play a pre-eminent part in the adolescent's daydreams and are representative of his expanding highly narcissistic sexual and aggressive strivings. Often the adolescent's egocentric attitudes and behavior, and his overconcern with values, interests, and pleasures which serve narcissistic-instinctual goals (self interests) rather than truly object-directed ones or aims of the superego, will appear superficial,

[1] Since wars mobilize sadistic and also narcissistic strivings and permit or even glorify them as long as they are subservient to the national ideal, it is not surprising that wars are regularly followed by an increase of juvenile delinquency.

[179]

irresponsible, and dangerous to the eyes of the adult beholder, who is not sufficiently aware of their significance in the adolescent's reconstruction of his superego and ego. It is true, of course, that the adolescent's fascination with these pseudo ideals and his acting out may, and frequently do, have very sad results. But as long as they remain within normal limits, the temporary efflorescence of such "worldly" interests and ambitions is indicative of the advancing instinctual, physical, mental, and intellectual maturation processes. Actually it has a most stimulating effect on ego development. The ultimate result is a gradual modification of the superego, with partial delegation of superego functions to the ego. This becomes manifest in the adolescent's struggle with his problem of self esteem, which his overconcern with the value of these new goals enlarges and extends from the moral sphere to all fields of physical, sexual, intellectual, and social accomplishments— a struggle in which he may succeed or fail.

To understand these problems, we should also realize that the adolescent's rapid growth and change necessitate continuous readjustments in his self representations. This makes the testing of his momentary psychic and bodily reality, and even of his physical and mental potentialities, extremely difficult.

Thus, it is not surprising that at this stage intense shame and inferiority conflicts make their appearance, in conjunction with painful guilt conflicts, betraying the sadistic quality which the superego temporarily acquires. The adolescent's shame and inferiority conflicts reveal that his vacillations of self esteem originate not only in moral conflicts but also in more primitive narcissistic conflicts: discordances between images of the grown-up, powerful, glamorous, brilliant, or sophisticated person he wants to be and sometimes believes himself to be, and the undeniable aspect of the physically and mentally immature, unstable, half-baked creature between two worlds, which he actually is. It is the mixture of moral conflicts with those of shame and inferiority that is responsible for the fluctuations in his identity feelings. Since these more primitive narcissistic conflicts induced by the temporary regressions and the resulting disorganization of the psychic structures cause not only loss of moral esteem but a total loss of self esteem, they may expand his moral and castration fears to regressive fears of loss of the total self. Frequently the adolescent's shame and inferiority conflicts may overshadow his guilt conflicts or be used as a disguise for them; but we can also observe the reverse. In other cases, as in the one to which I referred in Chapter 9, guilt conflicts may alternate and interact with shame and inferiority conflicts. All these conflicts will subside to the extent to which the adolescent's growing ego can get a grip on them.

Characteristically, in late adolescence boys and girls are preoccupied, either simultaneously or alternately, with highly valued "worldly" aims and "superficial" pleasures, with questions of appearance, manners, and formal behavior, and with very serious ethical and intellectual problems. In all these matters, they may suddenly seize upon a burning interest and an outspoken position, which may be dropped after some time and replaced by another one. Anna Freud (1936) has described these phenomena very beautifully. The efforts made by adolescents to form and formulate opinions, ideas, and ideals of their own gradually lead to the development of what we call a *Weltanschauung*. It is significant that this term refers merely to the way we "view the world," which is clearly a concern of the ego. In fact, our *Weltanschauung* covers a much broader field than our moral principles. It includes and determines our values, ideals, and ethical standards, but also extends to our opinions on nature and culture,

[181]

on sexual, social, racial, national, religious, political, and general intellectual problems.

The development of a *Weltanschauung* in adolescence indicates, indeed, that the ego and its preconscious and conscious thought processes can gradually begin to exert a considerable influence on both the superego and the id.

This once again leads us back to the superego identifications. The evolution of a *Weltanschauung* rests on the establishment of identifications with realistic parental figures, who within certain limits grant not only instinctual and emotional freedom but also freedom of thought and action. But this very freedom of thought has a curious dual effect on the further remodeling of the psychic systems. I have spoken of the adolescent's inclination to adore, idealize, and identify himself with new persons, who may be more suitable for such purposes than his parents. However, as his thought processes mature and become liberated, he will increasingly seek the company of persons and join social, athletic, political, cultural, or religious groups that will stimulate his own thinking and either share or instill in him new views, ideas, and ideals reflecting the ideational trends of "the coming generation." Whatever these trends may be, even if they are extreme and opposed to the opinions held by parents and school, new and potentially valuable personal and group identifications will develop on this advanced basis. They will ultimately support the reintegration of the superego and of those ego defenses which curtail and limit the liberties acquired in the course of adolescence. On the other hand, however, the liberation and maturation of thinking are bound to bring about an even further reduction of the role of identifications, inasmuch as they favor and reflect the adolescent's final establishment of ego and superego autonomy. The latter eventually brings about an increasing degree of freedom not only from external (parental and other personal, social, and cultural) influences but likewise from outmoded internal (instinctual as well as superego) pressures.

To be sure, for years we will also find unmistakable evidence of precisely the reverse: that id and superego in their turn find open gates to each other and to the ego, and gain a strong foothold in the thought processes. In fact, superego and id may infiltrate the ego to such an extent that the *Weltanschauung* may represent no more than a rationalization of either or both. Here I wish to refer again to Anna Freud's views (1936), and also to Heinz Hartmann's Freud Anniversary Lecture (1960), which are highly relevant to the issues under discussion. Thus, for long periods an adolescent's philosophy of life may vacillate in an almost preposterous way between opposing trends, depending on the predominant influence of either superego or id on his thinking. At one time he may surprise his liberal parents and teachers with puritanic, conservative, or reactionary opinions on moral, social, or political matters; and some months later he will suddenly shock them with revolutionary or hedonistic convictions, which afford evidence of his need for rationalizations, justifications, and glorifications of his irrepressible instinctual and selfish wishes and behavior.

In discussing the adolescent's asceticism, Anna Freud (1936) pointed out that his estrangement from the family seems to extend to the ego's attitude toward the superego, which is treated as though it were the forbidden incestuous love object. This is certainly correct. But we may further advance our understanding if, in addition, we take into consideration that these defensive attitudes of the ego toward the superego are part of the adolescent's desperate struggle for freedom and for independent individuality, and hence an expression of the ego's rebellious refusal to submit to any

[183]

authority or influence, be it from without or from within.

In fact, during periods of asceticism, as much as at stages when the adolescent professes hedonistic philosophies, he repersonifies and treats any part of the self—that is, not only the superego but also the id—as though they were powerful infantile love objects from whose prohibitive or seductive influence the ego must escape and of which the ego must rid itself. Obviously, during such periods the ego calls on early infantile defenses, such as isolation, denial, and gross projections, rather than repression, to ward off overwhelming pressures of the superego and the id (Jacobson, 1957). Thus it may happen that the adolescent's views, whatever they are at the time, become strangely disconnected from his instinctual and guilt conflicts and from behavior that may actually reveal either the irresistible force of his id or the sadistic power of his superego, whose hold on the ego cannot be tolerated.

While during this phase of transition the adolescent is naturally apt to employ external representatives whose philosophy he may temporarily accept, borrow, or oppose, he may likewise insist that his opinions are free of such external influences and reflect his own independent thinking. Actually, for a long time he may not be able to achieve more than a pretense of independence, maintained with the aid of such denial and isolation mechanisms.

To the adult environment these attitudes become especially exasperating at times when the adolescent subjects his problems to open discussion with his peers and sometimes to violent quarrels with parents, teachers, and other persons in authority. It is characteristic that in such arguments he will always defend his new convictions with the greatest vigor and often with superior, self-righteous, or even arrogant attitudes toward his adult opponent. This behavior actually reveals his underlying insecurity, suggestibility, and change-ability.

It is not surprising that, concomitantly with these hectic beginnings of a *Weltanschauung,* we observe in so many adolescents a flourishing of sublimations and of creative urges and activities which may fade out again after maturity has been reached.

Anna Freud (1936) has pointed out that instinctual danger stimulates the growth of intelligence in the adolescent as much as in the small child. But it is my impression that during this particular adolescent phase, when ego, superego, and id communicate so freely with each other, a singular dynamic, economic, and structural situation arises which is in many ways reminiscent of the conditions we may find in creative adults.

Of course, during all of adolescence the psychic organization is in a state of fluidity as never before or after. However, at the stage of tremendous instinctual-narcissistic inflation, when lasting defenses and countercathexes have not yet been re-established but when the ego's heroic efforts at leadership begin to meet with success, we may witness the development of a fluid interplay between primary- and secondary-process functioning. This interplay appears to be especially favorable to creative intellectual or artistic activity.

Provoked at first by the instinctual upheaval of this period and by the adolescent's need for orientation and guidance in the threatening world of adults, the development of a consistent and effective *Weltanschauung* is, of course, a process that continues after adolescence—indeed, through life. I need hardly emphasize to what extent the superego and id may still exercise their influence on the philosophy of adults, and even color their scientific convictions.

However, in late adolescence there occurs a slow but unmistakable shift of power to the ego, whose gain of strength manifests itself in its increasing influence on id and superego, causing a partial reversal of the situation. The ego now plays, as it were, the role of an active mediator. It employs the adolescent's worldly strivings and his identifications with realistic images of his parents and other "grownups" as aids for the toning down and readjustment of the superego and its moral codes, but then conversely calls on the latter for assistance in restricting the id and in developing mature ego goals and adult achievement standards. The ego's contribution to the restructuring of ego ideal and superego, and to the concomitant curbing of the adolescent's excessive instinctual and narcissistic expectations, slowly bridges the gaps and contradictions between his moral and worldly trends. In increasingly close collaboration, superego and ego thus gradually build up new sets of values which provide him with realistic goals and with consistent moral and other directives for the future.

This advance finds expression in the substance and solidity of the adolescent's judgment, views, and position in various worldly and intellectual matters and in the maturity, stability, and growing effectiveness of his ideals, his moral principles, and ethical convictions.

In view of the ego's role in the development of adult scales of value, we may well ask whether it would not be more correct to consider the ego ideal an ego formation rather than a part of the superego system. This was, indeed, suggested by Bing, McLaughlin, and Marburg (1959, p. 26). Probably for similar reasons Erikson (1956), too, delimits the superego from the ego ideal, which he regards as a more mature formation, while he does not sufficiently take into account the structural and functional alteration and development of the superego system as a whole during adolescence.

[186]

In my discussion of the shame conflicts I have already stressed that from the genetic and functional points of view the idea of separating the ego ideal from the morally prohibitive, enforcing, and critical superego is, indeed, not feasible, since they undeniably represent a functional unit and arise and develop as such. However, there is some merit to the reasoning of Bing, McLaughlin, and Marburg (1959). Although the ego ideal originates in the child's identifications with idealized parental images, it can certainly not be dissociated from the more and more individualized conscious value concepts and ideals which are built up during and after adolescence under the growing influence of the autonomous ego.

I believe that this dilemma in theory can be resolved when we understand that, because of the interaction between superego and ego, caused by the increase of ego identifications with realistic images of the adults and by the concomitantly receding role of identifications in favor of autonomous thought processes in general, the ego ideal during this phase gradually bridges the two systems and may ultimately be claimed by both.

In fact, the final stages in the development of the ego ideal demonstrate beautifully the hierarchic reorganization and final integration of different—earlier and later—value concepts, arising from both systems, into a new coherent structural and functional unit. At the same time we must realize that this reconstruction of the ego ideal can proceed only in conjunction and close interrelationship with the remodeling of the entire superego system and of its directive, enforcing, and critical functions, and with a corresponding growth of the ego's capacity for critical and self-critical moral and intellectual judgment.

Evidently the ultimate evolution of the ego ideal as a

coherent bridge structure connecting and belonging to both systems gradually permits the ego to support, supplant, and supplement superego functions. Subsequently, under the influence of its adjunct, the ego, the superego's operational methods become enriched and endowed with new individual features and with a variability and flexibility which the infantile superego lacks. Inasmuch as the superego regulates all human adjustment and social behavior, and the self-critical ego assists our practical adaptation to society and our mastery of reality, the growing harmony between the moral and ethical standards of the superego and the reality-directed goals of the ego will eventually facilitate the desirable, smooth, and intimate collaboration between the superego and corresponding ego functions, to which I referred in Chapter 9.

Concomitantly with this development, the superego fears and the fears induced by shame and inferiority conflicts are toned down, become less archaic-sadistic in their content and qualities, and will in part, at least, be replaced by more realistic anticipation of danger, such as Schur (1953, 1958) has described in various papers. In the case of normal development this results in a far greater ability of the ego to cope with intersystemic and intrasystemic conflicts.

Thus we see that these modifications in the superego and ego structures and functions ultimately lead to a remarkable strengthening of both systems. This enables the ego to reset and resolidify its defense organization, despite and precisely because of the fact that these modifications result in the attainment of instinctual freedom, freedom of object choice, of thought, feeling and action, and of greater freedom from external influences and from infantile id and superego pressures. In fact, all these liberties can be gained only to the extent to which superego and ego acquire sufficient autonomy and strength to subject them to the necessary limitations and to establish and maintain a stable and durable control system which is in accord with adult reality.

The special colors of the adolescent emotional and mood phenomena reflect the processes which I have discussed. Evidently the adolescent's erratic emotional vacillations mirror his swings from temporary disorganization, drive deneutralization and regression, causing a partial dissolution of old psychic structures, to dramatic mental progression leading to preponderance of the libidinous forces and drive reneutralization and to a restructuring and reorganization of the psychic systems. In the course of his mental trips back and forth, the adolescent will repeatedly be forced to make stops at various changing infantile levels and to re-establish primitive narcissistic types of object relations and identifications, which may reanimate fantasies of merging with objects (Geleerd, 1961).

When we give sufficient consideration to these processes, we understand that adolescent states of depression and elation can have multiple meanings and very different causes, and hence involve a great variety of conflicts and mechanisms. An adolescent's unhappiness may express his grief about childhood objects and pursuits that he must relinquish; his sadness may be tinged with painful longings, because he can neither go back to them nor yet reach new levels of achievement, of personal investments and pleasures. He may be depressed because he cannot gain the love of a girl he woos, or because he has failed in his work or in other pursuits and feels physically and personally inadequate, intellectually and mentally inferior and immature. But at other times his depression may be caused by guilt conflicts, either from sexual sources or because of his disproportionate, severe hostility. His depressive moods may at one time be devoid of regressive features, and at other times involve a retreat to homosexual or sadomasochistic positions, or even be expressive of a hostile and deeply narcissistic withdrawal from the world. Moreover, for the sake of his mental growth, the adolescent needs periods of quiet retreat and introspection, when he feels neither depressed nor lonely but wishes to indulge in solitude and take account of himself. The same variety of causes can be observed in the adolescent's states of happiness and elation. They may originate merely in loving or enthusiastic approaches to new interests, to the opposite sex, or to other new persons. But they may also be the aftermath of success, of narcissistic-aggressive conquest and victory in the area of work, of love and sex, accomplishments which show him that he has definitely reached a new developmental level.

From the economic point of view, we must take into account the adolescent's tendency to suffer from sporadic outbursts of aggression as much as from libidinal tempests. One day he may feel ready to die of sexual starvation, while on the next he may feel consumed by hate and self hate, and then again he may pour love from every niche of his soul upon others and on himself. He may be noisily joyful when he can discharge surplus libido in gay company or in flirtations and sexual play with youngsters. At times these parties may lead to wild activities, such as races in cars or motorboats, which offer an outlet for his excess aggression. More normally he exhausts himself in seasonal sports, games, and the like. At a stage in which large amounts of surplus hostility have been mobilized, his boundless aggression toward the world or himself may threaten the adolescent with inner object loss and loss of the self, whereas the influence of libidinal storms may result in his experiencing himself and the world as tremendously rich.

Because of this emotional intensity, some teenagers may be so all-absorbed by a mood that it may for weeks or longer

[190]

set their minds stubbornly and exclusively on one problem or activity or preoccupation.

"Last summer," I was told by the mother of an attractive, lively, intelligent girl of seventeen, "nothing but poetry existed for June. During the winter her only interests were dancing, flirtations, and boys. This summer she has spent sitting on the rocks, gazing dreamily at the ocean. . . ." It is characteristic that this was a girl who graduated from high school at sixteen and was an excellent, serious college student.

During stages when he feels overpowered by libidinal desires but equally afraid of homosexual and heterosexual attachments, the adolescent may indeed prefer lovingly to embrace mankind and its many causes instead of an individual, to indulge in ecstatic religious experiences of mystical union with God, or to celebrate lonely orgies with nature, poetry, music or art.

Such adolescent states certainly remind one of similar experiences which we can observe in schizophrenics. In the schizophrenic, as in the adolescent, such ecstatic experiences involve fantasies of merging with objects, which may be accompanied by rich self feelings. However, in the psychotic these feelings have a spurious quality and are frequently accomplished by mystic experiences of revelation and ideas of grandeur. The adolescent's states of ecstasy certainly epitomize the intensification of his narcissism. But they expand his self lovingly into the object world and endow both with those floods of libido which have been liberated and cannot yet be attached to new individual objects. Moreover, in contrast to such experiences in psychotics, these states may pass swiftly each time, to be followed by a sober return to reality and to everyday life activities. Evidently ecstatic states in nonpsychotic adults are of the same nature and develop for similar reasons.

No doubt, the long period of narcissistic overexpansion,

of concern with ambitious goals and highly narcissistic values, has a dangerous potential and accounts for the adolescent's propensity to such elated and depressive mood conditions. It is the depth of their narcissistic regressions which may, even in adolescents who are not grossly disturbed, cause transient depressive states with paranoid and hypochondriacal features, with feelings of utter loneliness and isolation, and with identity problems reminiscent of psychotic types of depression.

However, to our amazement we sometimes see that small events and experiences, which appear irrelevant on the surface, may suddenly and swiftly sweep away not only the depressive mood but all these alarming symptoms. They may recur, but may ultimately disappear without leaving any traces.

To the extent to which the adolescent's search for new love objects and for a new grown-up self meets with success, the fluctuations between periods of narcissistic expansion, of sexual and aggressive storms, and opposite phases of instinctual and narcissistic restriction and constriction will indeed subside. Subsequently the adolescent will be able to assert himself as an autonomous, grown-up, and sexually mature person, and create and accept a corresponding consistent and durable self representation. To the extent to which his sexual, narcissistic, and ambivalence conflicts, the vacillations of his self esteem and his identity conflicts pass, he will reach new and more object-directed aims and positions. Especially after he begins to permit himself heterosexual genital activities, he will feel ready to embark on more enduring and profound love relations, and to approach the problem of his future vocation in a realistic manner. When the adolescent has reached this level, toward the end of adolescence, we may say that he has found himself.

With full maturation and the achievement of instinctual mastery, the representations of the self and of the object world in general acquire a final, characteristic configuration. When we compare and confront these formations with each other, we find that in a "normal" person they have what may be called "complementary" qualities which characterize a prominent aspect of his personality. When we designate somebody, for instance, as an "optimist" (A. Katan, 1934), we mean that he regards himself as a lucky person, that he always expects to be successful and to gain gratification easily, and that he views the world as bound to be good and pleasurable and to treat him well. In harmony with these concepts he will be a person inclined to be hopeful, gay, and in good spirits. By contrast, the "pessimist" will experience the world as a constant source of harm, disappointment, and failure, and himself accordingly as a poor devil, forever apt to be deprived and hurt; consequently, the level of his mood will be preponderantly low. These examples show that, in a mature individual, these complementary qualities of his object and self representations reflect and define both his own identity and his *Weltbild*, i.e., his fundamental position in relation to himself and to the world. The fact that in the course of life this position may undergo further radical changes indicates that even after maturation and stabilization our concepts of the object world and of our own self may be profoundly influenced and altered by our life experiences and the biological stages through which we pass.

12

The Influence of Normal and Unsuccessful Adolescent Conflict Solution on Postadolescent Identity Formation and the Further Development of Personality

AFTER ADOLESCENCE, ego development proceeds less and less along the lines of identifications and grants increasing room to independent critical and self-critical judgment and to the individual, autonomous trends of the ego and its Anlage. I believe this is what Erikson (1956) alludes to when he says that *"Identity formation . . . begins where the usefulness of identification ends"* (p. 113). It is certainly true that at the stage when the adolescent begins to choose the direction in which he wishes to proceed, he may pass through identity experiences which have a significantly new and convincing quality (Eissler, 1957).

These experiences indicate that the process of identity formation is taking a new turn. However, in spite of the fact that the normal young adult is growing away from the family in which he was reared, and sooner or later will found a family of his own, his relations and identifications with persons of the past do not by any means ever "end." Actually, identity formation during the postadolescent stage of development and a person's future self realization depend not only on his liberation from the incestuous and dependency bonds of the past. No doubt, this liberation and the concomitantly receding role of identifications constitute preconditions for the further advance of the ego and superego autonomy and maturation, and hence for his ultimate identity formation. But the latter also rests on further successful modification, stabilization, and integration of the relations and identifications with persons of the past and on the resulting capacity for the establishment of sound, new selective personal and group relations and identifications. Both these factors, in conjunction, favor a flexible and free, but consistent and well-directed emotional and sexual, vocational and social development in the future.

This emphasizes the fact that we must not underrate the role which identification processes even normally continue to play in the further development of the human personality. The adolescent boy's fundamental and leading identifications with his father as a man later on extend quite naturally to his position as a husband and father, and may or may not determine the young man's vocational choice. Of course, this choice is only too often influenced by the father's ambitions, by his achievement standards and his narcissistic identifications with his son. Such attitudes may be the expression of the parents' reluctance to relinquish their own symbiotic ties to their child. This may arouse considerable conflict in childhood if the child's natural inclinations lie in fields of interest that appear undesirable to the parents, because they are different from the latter's expectations.

In the girl, likewise, the identifications with her mother gain considerably in strength after marriage, especially during pregnancy and her beginning motherhood. Here we again recall the parents' continuously changing identifications with their child and with their own parents, whose

[195]

significant role Benedek (1959) has described so impressively. Nor must we forget the identifications which marital partners may establish with each other during long years of marriage, to the point where they may even physically resemble each other. These mutual marital identifications may include the formation not only of the same life habits, the same routine of life, but also of the same ideals and the same set of standards—in other words, the same *Weltanschauung*, an issue that is of particular importance for the upbringing of their children.

But the part played by identification processes in the life of the adult does not remain limited to his past and future family. In connection with the adolescent's struggle for a *Weltanschauung*, I spoke of his need at this stage of great insecurity to derive narcissistic reinforcement of and stimulation for his own thought processes from identifications with social and cultural groups which are representative of the trend of his generation. During the postadolescent period these group activities and adherences will recede to the extent to which the individual's vocational, personal, and family life will shape and absorb his interests.

Yet group relations and group identifications do not by any means cease at this point to exert a significant influence on adult development. As the processes of final hierarchic organization in the various fields of the psychic arena set in, they will partly shift again to new groups and develop further. Thus the adult has specific relations and identifications not only with his class and with the racial and national groups to which he belongs but also with the vocational and social, political and scientific or religious groups which he may decide to join. Needless to say, such group identifications may serve a person to a greater or lesser degree as an effective frame of reference for his life, and frequently find remarkable

[196]

expression in his ideology and ideals, and in his way of living.

These different group relations, group identifications, and group adherences influence the individual's views, ideals, and standards, his behavior and role in the society in which he lives (his "ego identity"). In some of our patients, however, the group identifications and group relations may be in sharp conflict with each other, so that their reconciliation and integration may present extraordinary problems. Such persons usually manifest conspicuous identity conflicts. Their narcissistic attitudes and behavior, rapid emotional vacillation, inconsistency and changeability of their scales of value, and the dependency of their opinions on their current environment, or their opposition to the latter, frequently show at first glance that these persons suffer from protracted adolescent problems.

This leads us to a consideration of the failures in the solution of adolescent conflicts and to the factors responsible for them. Of course, my brief discussion of characteristic pathological trends arising from unresolved adolescent conflicts will again be restricted to the area of object relations and identifications and of identity formation. It goes without saying that postadolescent problems in these areas have their origins in infantile conflicts; but because of the particular dangers inherent in the adolescent struggle, the influential factors on which I have repeatedly placed emphasis acquire special significance with regard to its final outcome.

Before discussing the pathology which may arise from these particular sources, however, I must make some comments on the relations of self esteem to self feeling, a subject whose discussion I deliberately postponed in my discussion of the guilt, shame, and inferiority conflicts. Clinical observations confirm, indeed, that intersystemic narcissistic conflicts, i.e., conflicts between superego and ego, or instinctual

[197]

conflicts, i.e., conflicts between ego and id, do not commonly induce serious identity conflicts. To put it more cautiously, they do not tend to arouse disturbances in the experience of identity to the point of feelings of loss of the self. The validity of this statement is borne out not only by the absence of severe identity conflicts in psychoneurotics (unless they show a conspicuous narcissistic personality structure) but especially by the symptomatology in melancholic-depressive states. Although such patients may suffer from severe ambivalence and guilt conflicts leading to withdrawal from the object world, and even to delusional ideas of moral worthlessness, they ordinarily do not develop disturbances in their feelings of identity beyond experiences of depersonalization. In psychoneurotics the identity conflicts usually are limited to problems of sexual identity. Quite in contrast to this, loss of self esteem caused by those primitive narcissistic conflicts which find expression in conspicuous shame and inferiority feelings tends to affect the identity feelings to a much more dangerous degree. In fact, patients who manifest pathological shame reactions and fears of exposure coupled with self consciousness not only commonly suffer from identity problems; their superego frequently shows an infantile rigidity and lack of autonomy, indicative of immaturity and fragility of the moral system. This fragility may make it prone to rapid processes of regressive deterioration, which will have a profoundly disorganizing effect on the ego and the object relations. Again this is epitomized by psychotics, this time by the type of schizophrenics in whose states of depression the guilt conflicts may be absent or recede in favor of paranoid fears of exposure, while feelings of shame and inferiority, self consciousness and fears or feelings of loss of identity frequently appear as a characteristic triad of symptoms.

Even though the superego of the melancholic, with his

[198]

insatiable needs for love and narcissistic supply from his love objects, has infantile traits and is exceedingly cruel, it still seems to work at a developmental, structural, and functional level advanced enough to prevent the type of narcissistic conflicts which, based on a regressive disintegration and dissolution of superego standards and ego goals, of ego identifications and object relations, may induce experiences of loss of identity. This potential danger increases not only to the extent to which the ego's capacity for reality testing fails but also to the degree to which the moral system and hence the defenses break down and give way to destructive instinctual and grandiose infantile-narcissistic aims and strivings.

Thus, it does not suffice to say that the establishment of stable libidinal object relations and of consistent, well-organized ego identifications, of mature ego goals and ego autonomy are the premises on which normal postadolescent identity formation rests. We must regard the successful modification and stabilization of the superego in adolescence and the resulting effective regulation of ego functions and object relations as a protection from the danger of a total collapse of (object and) self representations. Conversely, we may even say that by virtue of its influence on the ego and the goals of the ego, the formation and existence of an intact, autonomous, well-functioning superego safeguard the maintenance of normal identity feelings in the adult.

Occasionally we encounter persons who, having lost their health, their work, their money, their position, their social status and prestige, nevertheless do not collapse under the onslaught of such narcissistic assaults, because they find support from their intact ethical and moral codes. Quite in contrast to such rare persons, we may observe in people who are not guided by a firm, coherent set of mature ethical standards a pronounced predisposition to identity problems. In

[199]

fact, there are gifted and very capable persons with a devouring ambition and amazing careers, who give the appearance of strong personalities and a "strong ego" but who actually have deep-rooted identity problems, because of the particular defectiveness of their superego and the narcissistic structure and fragility of their ego.

Let me now discuss postadolescent problems which reveal failures in the solution of the adolescent struggles in the areas to which I have turned my attention: the object relations, the identifications, and the process of identity formation.

I shall begin with problems caused by discrepancies between the adolescent processes of instinctual and ego maturation. Since both may be irregular and, moreover, proceed at a different pace, the conflicts developing from such sources may create serious difficulties and exert an unfortunate influence on the restructuring of ego and superego. Sexual precocity accompanying a comparatively slow ego maturation may result in as many problems as retarded sexual development in concomitance with early ego maturation. In the first case, we often observe superego problems which may become manifest in delinquent and wayward tendencies; such youngsters may build up and sustain a reactive set of false values, a pseudo ideal which offers them no ethical guidance but leads them astray. In the second case, we may find a no less dangerous trend toward overintellectualization or obsessional preoccupations, often in conjunction with asceticism and excessive moralism. Later on, when nature makes its claims, this may suddenly give way to opposite attitudes and hence to uncontrolled behavior.

In a good many instances, however, the slow or irregular pace of ego and superego development is caused not by delayed maturation but by parental attitudes which resist the adolescent's efforts to loosen his bonds with his family and to gain the instinctual freedom and the freedom of feelings, thoughts, and actions which I have discussed. In this case he may violently rebel against the parents; but, unable to break away from them, he forever remains regressively fixated at the adolescent level of insoluble conflicts, vacillating between dependent- and aggressive-narcissistic trends.

Let me briefly discuss a few different personality types belonging to this category. In some of these cases, narcissistic object relations and primitive identifications with glorified objects continue to determine the direction of ego and super-ego development after adolescence, to the point of interfering with the final maturation of these systems and with genuine individual identity formation. Fighting their dependency trends, such persons may derogate their parents and turn away from them in adolescence, but as adults they continue to emulate and lean upon other persons and groups and unduly admire them until they again rebel, abandon them in rage and disappointment, and look for the next object to be glorified and emulated. The more erotized such dependent-narcissistic relations are, the more passive and aggressive homosexual conflicts will be involved in these attachments. During the adolescent years of liberation from the family we commonly observe rapidly passing conflicts of this kind. But whenever parents refuse to accept the impending final separation from their children in adolescence, chronic pathology is bound to develop.

Such patients are apt to sustain as adults a proclivity to devastating shame reactions from infantile sources; reactions that may lead to depressive states with occasional brooding about ineradicable memories of shameful or humiliating situations. Some of these patients manifest a strong preponderance of shame over guilt reactions and of social over superego fears. This may be indicative of an insufficient internalization

[201]

or a regressive re-externalization of both shame and guilt conflicts and of the patients' final fixation or regression to infantile scales of value during the adolescent period. Their social fears commonly reveal themselves in awkwardness of behavior, combined with those painful feelings of self consciousness which make a regular temporary appearance in adolescence; but if these feelings occur in adults, they are a characteristic expression of continuing identity problems.

To give a brief case example. A female patient developed at about twenty a prolonged state of depression, in which guilt feelings played only a minor role. But she suffered from severe feelings of shame about any sexual or aggressive impulses she might experience toward either sex and about her tendency to acute gastrointestinal disturbances; she also suffered from tormenting feelings of self consciousness and shame with regard to her external appearance and behavior, her modes of walking and talking, and her manual skills. In other words, her fears of exposure, her self consciousness, and her shame reactions were mainly centered in the areas in which the child at the age of about two to three experiences his first feelings of independence from his mother and develops his first ambitions and feelings of pride. I have emphasized the fact that this is the period when the child has his first I-experiences. This beautiful girl, who had no regular vocation and lived mainly on grandiose fantasies of being a glamorous actress, bitterly complained that she did not know what she really wanted, that she had no incentive, no true interest, no continuity, goal, or direction and that she was different from everybody else but did not have any individuality of her own.

This patient's personality development had indeed been arrested at a very early preoedipal-narcissistic level. After her return from a series of boarding schools and colleges (ranging from parochial-Catholic to overprogressive ones), where she had spent almost her entire childhood from the age of six, she had become enslaved to her mother and her grandparents. They spoiled her and at the same time thwarted all her attempts to establish an independent adult life of her own. Playing the role of "young Bohemian people in their twenties," they could not, under any circumstances, admit the existence of a grown-up daughter and granddaughter. The reason for the early abandonment of this child had been the impending divorce of her parents, who were both extremely narcissistic, selfish, and utterly confused persons, and who had never developed any consistent and mature scales of ethical values, or any empathy for the needs of their daughter. Her mother remarried twice, her father four times.

This case illuminates some significant points. It shows the combination of predominantly preoedipal-narcissistic character traits and conflicts and an ego and superego pathology characterized by lack of autonomy and defectiveness of their functions, by deficiency of moral codes, and by shallowness, immaturity, and inconsistency in the goals of the ego. It underscores, in addition, the relations of this pathology to the preponderance of shame experiences, self consciousness, and identity problems.

Gifted acting-out patients with such a narcissistic personality structure, if familiar with psychoanalytic terminology, will frequently try to account for their agonizing experiences of anxiety, shame, and inferiority by pointing to their "high ego ideal." This is often rather misleading. In studying these conflicts, we find that they do not actually refer to the ego ideal or, for that matter, to any true "ideal"; but, on the contrary, they relate to aggrandized, wishful self images. These patients will express primitive narcissistic desires, such as becoming the greatest and most potent lover, the most handsome and creative person in the world, the greatest connoisseur of art, acquiring great wealth, being exquisitely dressed, reaching the top of society, and so on. These are the cases in which grandiose, sexual and aggressive (pregenital-phallic), narcissistic-exhibitionistic strivings have either survived unchecked since childhood or became revived and so much intensified in adolescence that they have succeeded in entering and asserting themselves enduringly in the superego and the goals of the ego under the guise of an ideal. This "ideal" becomes easily reattached to correspondingly glamorous, prominent persons whose company is sought because their grandeur immediately imparts itself to the self (A. Reich, 1960).

In the past of such patients, we find narcissistic parental attitudes, which did not permit the child's normal individuation and adolescent liberation, and which may have interfered with the development and organization of these patients' ego and supergo identifications and with identity formation. Moreover, contradictory emotional and educational parental attitudes, which created confusions in the area of values, may have caused problems in the development and integration of these patients' personal and group relations and identifications. I have stated that at the beginning of latency such problems may lead to experiences of confusion, loneliness, isolation, and to early identity conflicts. During adolescence these conflicts are apt to become remobilized and greatly intensified. They will then disturb the restructuring of ego and superego, and prevent the final reconciliation between the opposing trends of the superego and the id. Subsequently this will interfere not only with the final establishment of a mature ego ideal, of stable ego goals, and of autonomous ego and superego functions, but also with the adult's further development of sound selective personal and group relations and identifications. Such persons will be unable to accept and share for any length of time the ethical, social, and cultural standards and attitudes of the groups in which they live. They may boast that they like to live as outsiders and deliberate individualists, whereas actually they feel that "they do not belong" and are in a continuous search for identity.

In some patients of this kind, their ambitiousness may acquire a painfully driving and obsessional superego quality, and be so structurally intertwined with moral perfectionism that they suffer from superego fears as much as from social fears; and not only moral failures, but failures in any sphere will evoke in them a harassing mixture of guilt with inferiority feelings and shame reactions. This is frequently caused by precocious internalization of overpowering ambitious parental standards and demands in all areas of achievement during the earliest stages in the development of ego ideal and ego goals, identifications which could not be eliminated or modified during adolescence and which have remained enduringly effective.

Such patients commonly display severely masochistic-dependent trends and a predisposition to depressive states which may alternate with or be covered up by aggressive narcissistic behavior.

Two male patients of this type lent themselves especially to a study of the significant role of object and self constancy in the establishment of a stable superego structure that can safeguard identity formation. Both patients were obsessional-compulsives who since adolescence had suffered from recurring paranoid states of depression with excruciating fears of exposure and humiliation. Both had a marked tendency to "fail in success."

These two patients were forever dissatisfied with the choice

[205]

of their wives and of their vocations, in which they were actually quite outstanding. They had always had regrets about their past and present situation, and were obsessionally preoccupied with ideas of a drastic change of their lives in the future. Each expressed the desire to be a genius because this would permit him the "complete freedom" he craved.

To any little disappointment or failure these men would react with an angry-depressive mood, blaming either their wives or their current work and environment for ruining their lives. Subsequently they would develop fantasies either about an interesting woman they had recently met, or about a fascinating new job for which they might exchange the one to which they were committed. Not only would they constantly dream of leaving their jobs and their families; several times they had actually turned to quite a different field of work and started extramarital affairs. However, when these desirable new objects of interest became accessible, the picture would soon become reversed. The new situation would appear to be a dangerous trap from which they would want to or did escape by returning to the old objects which suddenly regained the attractiveness they had lost for a period of time.

This symptomatic picture, the underlying ambivalence and dependency conflicts, and the vacillations between homosexual and heterosexual love objects, which motivated the patients' behavior, are rather familiar to us. What was unusual, however, was the disturbance of their feelings of identity, with which these patients reacted to the alterations or reversals of their emotional state. Having returned to an old object, interest, or situation, for example, they could hardly "remember" their past feeling state and not even empathize with their recent enthusiasm about the new object and their former angry-paranoid rejection of the old one.

They felt equally disconnected and estranged from whole periods in their past life when they had been deeply involved with persons and activities that they had later relinquished. They looked back to such past periods as though these had been experienced by a different person with whom they had nothing in common.

Both these patients had been reared in families that had lived in a constant state of war. One had lost his father in early childhood, the other in adolescence as a result of divorce. From childhood on, each had periodically deserted his mother for the father or for a father figure, and then ,egretfully returned to her until, in late adolescence, each had withdrawn almost completely from his family and displaced his acting out to new persons. Neither patient had ever succeeded in establishing true object constancy in terms of building up enduring representations of "good but also bad" parents. Hence they had never developed a stable love relationship with a woman, or lasting identifications with their fathers or father figures. They were in constant search for an "only good" object whose all-loving image would not collapse, but would help them to establish lasting self representations by virtue of building up enduring and consistent identifications.

·Of course, no object could live up to their expectations. When they felt disappointed in the current object of their choice, these patients would thus tend to desert it and to split off its "all bad" image completely from the wishful, "all good" one that now would be thrown on a new person or interest. Because of their regressive (introjective and projective) narcissistic identifications with these objects, the split into "only bad" (breastless and castrated) and "only good" (bisexual) images would impart itself to the image of their own selves. Hence, each such change in feeling, fantasy, or action from a bad to a good object would be associated with experiences of throwing off their pasts and acquiring new identities different and completely disconnected from those of the past, which could no longer even be "remembered" as being their own.

In these two cases, which call to mind M. Klein's (1934) studies of paranoid patients, one could observe how the inability to establish object and self constancy were reflected in the patients' superego and ego pathology: in the changes between periods of impulsive acting out and of obsessional-compulsive behavior; in the alternation of (heterosexual and homosexual) love objects and of ego interests; in the endless search for enduring relations and identifications, and for an enduring self; and, hence, in the experience of discontinuity and changes of their personal identity.

Patients with this kind of conflicts may be narcissistic-neurotic personality types, such as these two patients. A. Reich (1953, 1954, 1960) has studied and beautifully described such patients in several papers. Depending on the degree to which their superego functions are defective, they may display traits of delinquency and suffer mainly from fears of being caught. But whenever we find not only a preponderance of shame and inferiority feelings over guilt reactions, but a conspicuous absence of true guilt conflicts and their replacement with shame and inferiority conflicts and with paranoid fears of exposure, we are justified in suspecting regressive processes in the superego and ego, suggestive of borderline or paranoid schizophrenic conditions. Whatever the pathogenic role of constitutional factors or of the infantile history, psychotic illnesses begin so frequently in adolescence because of the dangerous part of regressive processes in the adolescent's search for new objects and a new self and because of the severity of his instinctual and ambivalence conflicts. Their mastery requires indeed an inherent potential strength of ego and superego, even if these conflicts stay in normal bounds.

When early experiences of severe disappointment and abandonment have prevented the building up of unambivalent object relations and stable identifications in childhood and weakened the child's self esteem and his belief in finding love in the future, the first disappointing attempts of the adolescent to turn to new love objects may result in severe ambivalence conflicts, causing depressive states. In case of a constitutional psychotic predisposition, these conflicts may then precipitate periodically recurring psychotic-depressive states with withdrawal from the object world.

But when children grow up in an atmosphere of emotional and spiritual poverty, either because their parents were pathologically narcissistic, unstable, confused, unable to love, and did not support the process of individuation and the development of consistent scales of values and of enduring object relations and identifications, the adolescent conflicts may provoke schizophrenic illnesses—depending, of course, upon the nature of the constitutional predisposition.

In such cases of schizophrenic regression and disintegration of the psychic systems, we observe that the moral system may disintegrate, object relations and ego identifications may dissolve and regress to pathological destructive fantasies of fusion with objects. These processes can lead to an irreversible collapse of object and self representations. The superego may then consist of disconnected or even fragmented imagistic components, which may be in conflict with each other. The superego as well as the ego functions which control self esteem will be completely out of gear and will constantly collide with each other. In these circumstances profound identity conflicts are bound to develop.

[209]

Some delinquent or certain acting-out paranoid psychotic patients may, as a result of the disintegration of superego codes and ego goals, develop either a sadistic-criminal or a glamorous-grandiose pseudo ideal, which is usually isolated from the unconscious severely punitive early infantile super-ego components and opposed to them. The latter will in turn be inconsistent and have the quality of frightening, sadistic, powerful personified object-self images, which may likewise oppose each other. The narcissistic and conflicting parental attitudes may be faithfully reflected in these contradictions.

The severe pathology of these patients merely caricatures what we occasionally observe in latency children (Jacobson, 1930) and commonly in adolescents who, struggling for liberation from an overrestrictive superego, glorify the instinctual freedom they want to attain.

I shall conclude my comments with a few brief case examples which demonstrate such psychotic pathology.

The disconnection of the cruelly threatening superego components from a conscious sexualized-perverse-aggressive gangster ideal and the way they worked at cross-purposes were especially conspicuous in a homosexual paranoid schizo-phrenic patient, who had been in a prepsychotic state from early childhood on. But only in adolescence did his inability to resolve his homosexual and ambivalence conflicts with his father precipitate manifest psychotic symptoms for the first time. He became an acting-out, polymorph-perverse, con-fused person, who suffered from intermittent paranoid-depressive and agitated states with mild delusional ideas of persecution and severely destructive and self-destructive impulses, leading to fears of world destruction and experi-ences of loss of self. During World War II, following a conflict with his superior officer in the Army, which led to a paranoid rage attack, he finally did cause an explosion in which he blinded himself and thereafter committed suicide by hanging himself.

The childhood history of this tragic case illuminated the disturbances of ego and superego development and of identity formation, which arise when identifications with unfavorable parental attitudes establish themselves too firmly and prematurely in the infantile ego and the superego precursors before the ego can attain a certain degree of strength and autonomy.

This patient had had a chronically sick mother, who had been absent during almost his entire childhood. From infancy on he had been brought up by a confused and very narcissistic father who not only showed a complete disregard for the child's needs and treated him as an extension of himself but alternated between severely prohibitive and exceedingly protective and seductive maternal attitudes. Because of the patient's prolonged close symbiosis with his father, the inconsistent attitudes of the latter had become prematurely and hence ineradicably engrained in the child. In such a case these attitudes get a firm foothold in the infantile ego, in the form of inescapable, controlling, threatening, prohibitive or seductive self-object images. They are experienced as a destructive parasitic foreign body of which the child tries in vain to rid himself, because he feels it has become an indelible part of his own self.

From the study of such patients we gain the impression that in their childhood the preoedipal superego forerunners have already been split up in an unusual, pathological manner. There may be a component reflecting the strict maternal —or paternal—demands, and an opposing part developing from reactive attempts to overthrow and expel the parasitic, sadistically controlling introjected parental images. This countermove, which in my patient had been promoted by contradictory paternal attitudes, will lead to the development of such conscious omnipotent-sadistic gangster "ideals" to which I referred above. The nature of such harmful, early, irreversible introjection processes has been sufficiently discussed in the literature. Less has been said about their influence on the ego and the ego identifications, which develop in such circumstances.

In general, maternal attitudes will impose themselves more easily and drastically on the total ego during the first childhood years. The more prolonged the child's dependency situation, and the deeper and more powerful the imprint of the mother's attitudes on the preoedipal forerunners of superego and ego ideal, the more will the parental influences, instead of gradually and selectively modifying the ego, interfere with, arrest, or even smother its autonomous development. They will invade, spread out, and pervade the whole personality and fixate it on a preoedipal level. The thus evolving ego will be characterized by predominance of narcissistic-parasitic features, of pregenital and sadomasochistic drive components, of their ego derivatives, and frequently of rigid but unstable reaction formation established against them. The more such a child tries to rebel against the parental intrusion, the more fragile and uneven will be the superego and ego structures. Of course, such a child will be unable to establish normal object relations, discriminate identifications and hence normal defenses and firm, consistent, countercathectic formations. In adolescence, such fragile ego and superego structures are bound to break down under the pressure of overpowering sexual and aggressive instinctual forces.

It is interesting that in cases where a sadistic mother image has been prematurely introjected, the ego identifications frequently develop along the lines of a masochistic maternal

[212]

image. In one of my patients, a severely sadomasochistic, paranoid-depressive girl who actually had an extremely sadistic, overpowering mother, the primal-scene fantasies pictured this sadistic mother as the victim of the cruel father. This masochistic concept, which found support in the mother's constant complaints about her husband, was the basis on which the patient's masochistic identifications and character formation rested.

With respect to the superego, such premature introjections of powerful parental images into the images of the self will in childhood sufficiently inhibit the maturation of those very functions which are a prerequisite for the formation of a coherent, mature, autonomous moral system. Consequently the superego—prematurely implanted and endowed with sadistic, pregenital qualities—has no opportunity of advancing to a higher level during childhood and adolescence. It will remain archaic and defective in its structure. For this reason it will never develop adequate signal, enforcing, and guiding functions that can promote the development of mature ego goals and of stable defenses, permitting normal personal relations and free functional ego activity.

The pathological results of such overpowerful maternal or parental influences on ego and superego development and identity formation certainly can be best observed in psychotic patients whose childhood history shows that their symbiotic union with the mother or with both parents had been stubbornly and forcefully maintained by the latter from birth to adulthood. In such patients the introjected parental images may dominate the ego in a totalitarian way as did once the powerful, omnipotent mother. The patients may frankly say that they feel as if the mother (or parents) have lived in them like parasites—on the one hand, as dangerous objects continuously threatening, commanding, forbidding,

[213]

punishing, or also protecting, seducing, and inciting, but on the other hand, as a parasitic ego which, smothering and replacing their own, feels or thinks or acts in their stead. We may learn from their childhood history that in the earliest years the ego had actually renounced its own independent development in favor of an all-pervasive emulation of parents, which completely dominated their sexual lives, feelings, thoughts, and actions.

I shall conclude with a brief case report on a brilliant boy who suffered his first psychotic paranoid break at the age of fifteen. His case illuminates the pathological processes to which I have referred. The boy's first acute episode developed after an infatuation with a beautiful girl who rejected him in favor of another boy friend. It is characteristic that the boy never seriously tried to approach her. His parents did not really notice that anything was amiss until they found a revolver in his bed. He had another break after entering college and had to quit school for a year. Although he never fully recovered, he was then able to re-enter college, to finish it at the age of twenty-three, and to go into his father's business. From then on he seemed to have made a fairly good adjustment, though on a lower level.

I observed and treated the boy between his eighteenth and twenty-third year. During this period he was unable to relate to his peers, either boys or girls, and vacillated between paranoid rages at his parents and other authorities and extreme submission, submersion in, and dependency on them. For years he maintained the paranoid conviction that all wives, including his mother, a school principal, tried to kill their husbands. His relations to the object world during these years were limited to homosexual or heterosexual sadomasochistic fantasies, in which he would alternately identify himself with sadistic dictators or with their victims. He frequently felt the urge either to rape and strangle girls on the street or to castrate himself. Outwardly he was extremely polite and formal, though he tried to imitate the behavior of admired schoolmates, mostly of the bully type. He was extremely self conscious, felt continuously observed, and was afraid of being exposed as a homosexual or a killer. Consequently he avoided social activities of any kind. His pathological pseudo relations to the object world interacted with severe identity conflicts. He complained bitterly that he did not know who he was and what he wanted, that he had no goals, no directions, no beliefs, and no ideals; that he was nobody and different from anybody else; that he never felt the same from one day to the next.

The boy's identity conflicts reflected those characteristic parental attitudes to which I have repeatedly referred. The parents were elderly people who had married at the end of their thirties. He was the only child. They were indeed both uniquely narcissistic; they had been dutiful parents but unloving and completely unaware of their child's needs, and exceptionally contradictory in their educational attitudes toward him. To give an example: the parents told me that when they caught their boy masturbating at the age of nine, they threatened him with future insanity and wept in front of him about their poor child's sexual precocity. From then on they constantly watched over him, accompanying him to the toilet; at the same time the mother put ointment on his "sore" penis every night, thus causing erections which led to obsessional masturbation with incestuous fantasies.

The mother admitted that she had never allowed the boy to play with other children outside their own home. But after another mother told her that she was "overprotective," he was sent alone from Westchester to New York on the following day, got lost, was frightened out of his wits, and was

[215]

almost run over by a car. These parents reported to me with great satisfaction how, from earliest childhood on, he had been "precisely the way we wanted him to be, precisely the way we are ourselves." This was true. Whereas he had never built up consistent and selective ego and superego identifications with his parents, he had so completely imitated and emulated his parents, and later on his teachers, that he had never known the pleasure of spontaneous, free ego activity. Until the age of fifteen, when he broke down, he had been a mixture of an overly dependent baby and a highly intelligent but rigidly compulsive-depressive character. The reason for the instability and fragility of his ego and superego structure, which caused the psychotic illness, was the overpowering hostility provoked, early in childhood, by the premature smothering of his ego autonomy, and the complete interference with a normal process of identity formation. This boy remembered fantasies, even at the age of seven, in which he saw himself strapped to his mother's breast, flying straight to hell. "I hated her so much that I wanted her to go to hell," he said, "but being chained to her, I had to go to hell with her." This sounded like a premonition. His psychotic episode in adolescence ensued from frantic efforts to rebel and to free himself by shaking off the intolerable burden of his enslavement, his inhibitions, his rigid reaction formations and compulsions, and by sending the overpowerful superego-ego-mother to hell. The result was chaos, and his breakdown did drive his mother to despair.

Bibliography

ABRAHAM, K. (1924), A Short Study of the Development of the Libido, Viewed in the Light of Mental Disorders. *Selected Papers on Psycho-Analysis.* London: Hogarth Press, 1949, pp. 418-501.

ALEXANDER, F. (1928), The Neurotic Character. *Int. J. Psycho-Anal.,* 11:292-311, 1930.

AXELRAD, S. & MAURY, L. M. (1951), Identification as a Mechanism of Adaptation. In: *Psychoanalysis and Culture,* ed. G. B. Wilbur & W. Muensterberger. New York: International Universities Press, pp. 168-184.

BAK, R. (1939), Regression of Ego Orientation and Libido in Schizophrenia. *Int. J. Psycho-Anal.,* 20:64-71.

—— (1949), The Psychopathology of Schizophrenia. *Bull. Amer. Psychoanal. Assn.,* 5:44-49.

BALINT, A. (1931), *The Early Years of Life.* New York: Basic Books, 1954.

—— (1943), Identification. *Int. J. Psycho-Anal.,* 24:97-107.

BALINT, M. (1937), Frühe Entwicklungsstadien des Ichs. Primäre Objektliebe, *Imago,* 23:270-288.

BENDER, L. (1953), *Aggression, Hostility and Anxiety in Children.* Springfield, Ill.: Thomas.

BENEDEK, T. (1949), The Psychosomatic Implications of the Primary Unit: Mother-Child. *Amer. J. Orthopsychiat.,* 19:642-654. (Republished as Chapter 12, in T. Benedek: *Psychosexual Functions in Women.* New York: Ronald Press, 1956.)

—— (1956), Toward the Biology of the Depressive Constellation. *J. Amer. Psychoanal. Assn.,* 4:389-427.

—— (1959), Parenthood as a Developmental Phase. *J. Amer. Psychoanal. Assn.,* 7:389-417.

BERES, D. (1958), Vicissitudes of Superego Functions and Superego Precursors in Childhood. *The Psychoanalytic Study of the Child,* 13:324-335. New York: International Universities Press.

—— & OBERS, S. J. (1950), The Effects of Extreme Deprivation in Infancy on Psychic Structure in Adolescence: A Study in Ego Development. *The Psychoanalytic Study of the Child*, 5:212-235. New York: International Universities Press.

BERGMAN, P. & ESCALONA, S. (1949), Unusual Sensitivities in Very Young Children. *The Psychoanalytic Study of the Child*, 3/4:333-352. New York: International Universities Press.

BERNFELD, S. (1931), Zur Sublimierungstheorie. *Imaago*, 17:399-403.

BING, J., MCLAUGHLIN, F., & MARBURG, R. (1959), The Metapsychology of Narcissism. *The Psychoanalytic Study of the Child*, 14:9-28. New York: International Universities Press.

BLOS, P. (1962), *On Adolescence: A Psychoanalytic Interpretation*. New York: Free Press of Glencoe.

BORNSTEIN, B. Quoted by N. Root (1957).

BOWLBY, J. (1958), The Nature of the Child's Tie to His Mother. *Int. J. Psycho-Anal.*, 39:350-373.

—— (1960), Grief and Mourning in Infancy and Early Childhood. *The Psychoanalytic Study of the Child*, 15:9-52. New York: International Universities Press.

BOYER, L. B. (1956), On Maternal Overstimulation of Ego Defects. *The Psychoanalytic Study of the Child*, 11:236-256. New York: International Universities Press.

DEUTSCH, H. (1944), *The Psychology of Women: A Psychoanalytic Interpretation*, Vol. I. New York: Grune & Stratton.

EIDELBERG, L. (1961), On Narcissistic Mortification. Abstracted in Panel: Narcissism, reported by J. F. Bing & R. O. Marburg. *J. Amer. Psychoanal. Assn.*, 10:593-605, 1962.

EISSLER, K. R. (1957), Problems of Identity. Abstracted in Panel: Problems of Identity, reported by D. L. Rubinfine. *J. Amer. Psychoanal. Assn.*, 6:131-142, 1958.

—— (1958), Notes on Problems of Technique in the Psychoanalytic Treatment of Adolescents. With Some Remarks on Perversions. *The Psychoanalytic Study of the Child*, 13:223-254. New York: International Universities Press.

ELKISCH, P. & MAHLER, M. S. (1959), On Infantile Precursors of the "Influencing Machine" (Tausk). *The Psychoanalytic Study of the Child*, 14:219-235. New York: International Universities Press.

ERIKSON, E. H. (1946), Ego Development and Historical Change. In: *Identity and the Life Cycle* [*Psychological Issues*, Monogr. 1]. New York: International Universities Press, 1959, pp. 18-49.

—— (1956), The Problem of Ego Identity. In: *Identity and the Life Cycle* [*Psychological Issues*, Monogr. 1]. New York: International Universities Press, 1959, pp. 101-166.

[218]

ESCALONA, S. (1952), Emotional Development in the First Year of Life. In: *Problems of Infancy and Childhood,* ed. M. J. E. Senn. New York: Josiah Macy, Jr., Foundation, pp. 11-91.

—— & Heider, G. M. (1959), *Prediction and Outcome: A Study in Child Development.* New York: Basic Books.

FEDERN, P. (1952), *Ego Psychology and the Psychoses.* New York: Basic Books.

FENICHEL, O. (1926), Identification. *The Collected Papers of Otto Fenichel,* 1:97-112. New York: Norton, 1953.

—— (1935), A Critique of the Death Instinct. *The Collected Papers of Otto Fenichel,* 1:363-372. New York: Norton, 1953.

—— (1937), Early Stages of Ego Development. *The Collected Papers of Otto Fenichel,* 2:25-48. New York: Norton, 1954.

—— (1945), *The Psychoanalytic Theory of Neurosis.* New York: Norton.

FISHER, C. (1954), Dreams and Perception: The Role of Preconscious and Primary Modes of Perception in Dream Formation. *J. Amer. Psychoanal. Assn.,* 3:389-445.

—— (1957), A Study of the Preliminary Stages of the Construction of Dreams and Images. *J. Amer. Psychoanal. Assn.,* 5:5-60.

—— & Paul, J. H. (1959), Subliminal Visual Stimulation and Dreams. *J. Amer. Psychoanal. Assn.,* 7:35-83.

FREUD, A. (1936), *The Ego and the Mechanisms of Defense.* New York: International Universities Press, 1946.

—— (1949), Aggression in Relation to Emotional Development: Normal and Pathological. *The Psychoanalytic Study of the Child,* 3/4:37-42. New York: International Universities Press.

—— (1958), Adolescence. *The Psychoanalytic Study of the Child,* 13:255-278. New York: International Universities Press.

—— (1960), Discussion of Dr. John Bowlby's Paper. *The Psychoanalytic Study of the Child,* 15:53-62. New York: International Universities Press.

FREUD, S. (1900), The Interpretation of Dreams. *Standard Edition,* 4 & 5. London: Hogarth Press, 1953.

—— (1905), Three Essays on the Theory of Sexuality. *Standard Edition,* 7:125-243. London: Hogarth Press, 1953.

—— (1914), On Narcissism: An Introduction. *Collected Papers,* 4:30-59. London: Hogarth Press, 1948.

—— (1915), The Unconscious. *Collected Papers,* 4:98-136. London: Hogarth Press, 1948.

—— (1917a), A Metapsychological Supplement to the Theory of Dreams. *Collected Papers,* 4:137-151. London: Hogarth Press, 1948.

—— (1917b), Mourning and Melancholia. *Collected Papers,* 4:152-170. London: Hogarth Press, 1948.

—— (1920), *Beyond the Pleasure Principle*. London: Hogarth Press, 1948.

—— (1923), *The Ego and the Id*. London: Hogarth Press, 1927.

—— (1924), The Economic Problem in Masochism. *Collected Papers*, 2:255-268. London: Hogarth Press, 1948.

—— (1925), Negation. *Collected Papers*, 5:181-185. London: Hogarth Press, 1950.

—— (1926), *Inhibitions, Symptoms and Anxiety*. London: Hogarth Press, 1948.

—— (1931), Female Sexuality. *Collected Papers*, 5:252-272. London: Hogarth Press, 1950.

—— (1932), *New Introductory Lectures on Psychoanalysis*. New York: Norton, 1933.

—— (1940), *An Outline of Psychoanalysis*. New York: Norton, 1948.

FRIES, M. E. (1935), Interrelationship of Physical, Mental and Emotional Life of a Child from Birth to Four Years of Age. *Amer. J. Dis. Child,* 45:1546-1563.

—— (1944), Psychosomatic Relationships between Mother and Infant. (From the Proceedings of the Conference on the Psychosomatic Status of the Infant at Birth.) *Psychosom. Med.,* 6:159-162.

—— & LEWI, B. (1938), Interrelated Factors in Development: A Study of Pregnancy, Labor, Delivery, Lying-in Period, and Childhood. *Amer. J. Orthopsychiat.,* 8:726-752.

GELEERD, E. R. (1958), Borderline States in Childhood and Adolescence. *The Psychoanalytic Study of the Child,* 13:279-295. New York: International Universities Press.

—— (1961), Some Aspects of Ego Vicissitudes in Adolescence. *J. Amer. Psychoanal. Assn.,* 9:394-405.

GLOVER, E. (1939), *Psychoanalysis: A Handbook for Medical Practitioners and Students of Comparative Psychology*. London: Staples Press.

GREENACRE, P. (1948), Anatomical Structure and Superego Development. In: *Trauma, Growth and Personality*. New York: Norton, 1952, pp. 149-164.

—— (1950), Special Problems of Early Female Sexual Development. In: *Trauma, Growth and Personality*. New York: Norton, 1952, pp. 237-258.

—— (1958), Early Physical Determinants in the Development of the Sense of Identity. *J. Amer. Psychoanal. Assn.,* 6:612-627.

GREENSON, R. R. (1954), The Struggle against Identification. *J. Amer. Psychoanal. Assn.,* 2:200-217.

—— (1958), Screen Defenses, Screen Hunger, and Screen Identity. *J. Amer. Psychoanal. Assn.,* 6:242-262.

[220]

—— (1960), Empathy and Its Vicissitudes. *Int. J. Psycho-Anal.*, 41:418-424.

GRINKER, R. (1955), Growth, Inertia and Shame: Their Theoretical Implications and Dangers. *Int. J. Psycho-Anal.*, 36:242-253.

—— (1957), On Identification. *Int. J. Psycho-Anal.*, 38:379-390.

HARTMANN, H. (1939), *Ego Psychology and the Problem of Adaptation.* New York: International Universities Press, 1958.

—— (1950), Comments on the Psychoanalytic Theory of the Ego. *The Psychoanalytic Study of the Child*, 5:74-96. New York: International Universities Press.

—— (1952), The Mutual Influences in the Development of Ego and Id. *The Psychoanalytic Study of the Child*, 7:9-30. New York: International Universities Press.

—— (1955), Notes on the Theory of Sublimation. *The Psychoanalytic Study of the Child*, 10:9-29. New York: International Universities Press.

—— (1960), *Psychoanalysis and Moral Values* [The Freud Anniversary Lecture Series, The New York Psychoanalytic Institute]. New York: International Universities Press.

—— KRIS, E., & LOEWENSTEIN, R. M. (1946), Comments on the Formation of Psychic Structure. *The Psychoanalytic Study of the Child*, 2:11-38. New York: International Universities Press.

—— —— —— (1949), Notes on the Theory of Aggression. *The Psychoanalytic Study of the Child*, 3/4:9-36. New York: International Universities Press.

—— & LOEWENSTEIN, R. M. (1962), Notes on the Superego. *The Psychoanalytic Study of the Child*, 17:42-81. New York: International Universities Press.

HENDRICK, I. (1943), The Discussion of the "Instinct to Master." A Letter to the Editors. *Psychoanal. Quart.*, 12:561-565.

—— (1951), Early Development of the Ego: Identification in Infancy. *Psychoanal. Quart.*, 20:44-61.

HERMANN, I. (1929), Das Ich und das Denken. *Imago*, 15:325-348.

—— (1936), Sich-Anklammern, Auf-Suche-Gehen. *Int. Z. Psychoanal.*, 22:349-370.

HOFFER, W. (1949), Mouth, Hand and Ego-Integration. *The Psychoanalytic Study of the Child*, 3/4:49-56. New York: International Universities Press.

ISAKOWER, O. (1939), On the Exceptional Position of the Auditory Sphere. *Int. J. Psycho-Anal.*, 20:340-348.

JACOBSON, E. (1930), Beitrag zur asozialen Charakterbildung. *Int. Z. Psychoanal.*, 16:210-235.

—— (1937), Wege der weiblichen Über-Ich-Bildung. *Int. Z. Psychoanal.*, 23:402-412.

—— (1953a), The Affects and Their Pleasure-Unpleasure Qualities in Relation to the Psychic Discharge Processes. In: *Affects, Drives, Behavior*, ed. R. M. Loewenstein. New York: International Universities Press, pp. 38-66.

—— (1953b), Contribution to the Metapsychology of Cyclothymic Depression. In: *Affective Disorders*, ed. P. Greenacre. New York: International Universities Press, pp. 49-83.

—— (1954a), The Self and the Object World. *The Psychoanalytic Study of the Child*, 9:75-127. New York: International Universities Press.

—— (1954b), Contribution to the Metapsychology of Psychotic Identification. *J. Amer. Psychoanal. Assn.*, 2:239-262.

—— (1957), Denial and Repression. *J. Amer. Psychoanal. Assn.*, 5:61-92.

—— (1959), Depersonalization. *J. Amer. Psychoanal. Assn.*, 7:581-610.

JEKELS, L. (1930), Zur Psychologie des Mitleids. *Imago*, 16:5-22.

—— (1936), Mitleid und Liebe. *Imago*, 22:383-388.

JOSSELYN, I. (1954), Ego in Adolescence. *Amer. J. Orthopsychiat.*, 24:223-237.

KANZER, M. (1962), Ego Interest, Egoism and Narcissism. Abstracted in Panel: Narcissism, reported by J. H. Bing & R. O. Marburg. *J. Amer. Psychoanal. Assn.*, 10:593-605.

KATAN, A. (1934), Einige Bemerkungen über Optimismus. *Int. Z. Psychoanal.*, 20:191-199.

—— (1937), The Role of "Displacement" in Agoraphobia. *Int. J. Psycho-Anal.*, 32:41-50, 1951.

KLEIN, M. (1934), A Contribution to the Psychogenesis of Manic-Depressive States. In: *Contributions to Psycho-Analysis, 1921-1945*. London: Hogarth Press, 1948, pp. 282-310.

KNIGHT, R. P. (1940), Introjection, Projection and Identification. *Psychoanal. Quart.*, 9:334-341.

KRAMER, P. (1955), On Discovering One's Identity: A Case Report. *The Psychoanalytic Study of the Child*, 10:47-74. New York: International Universities Press.

—— (1958), One of the Preoedipal Roots of the Superego. *J. Amer. Psychoanal. Assn.*, 6:38-46.

KRIS, E. (1952), *Psychoanalytic Explorations in Art*. New York: International Universities Press.

—— (1955), Neutralization and Sublimation: Observations on Young Children. *The Psychoanalytic Study of the Child*, 10:30-46. New York: International Universities Press.

LAMPL-DE GROOT, J. (1937). Masochismus und Narzissmus. *Int. Z. Psvchoanal.*, 23:479-489.

—— (1947), On the Development of the Ego and Superego. *Int. J. Psycho-Anal.*, 23:7-11.

—— (1960), On Adolescence. *The Psychoanalytic Study of the Child*, 15:95-103. New York: International Universities Press.

LEWIN, B. D. (1950), *The Psychoanalysis of Elation*. New York: Norton.

LICHTENSTEIN, H. (1961), Identity - and Sexuality: A Study of Their Interrelationships in Man. *J. Amer. Psychoanal. Assn.*, 9:179-260.

—— (1963), The Dilemma of Human Identity: Notes on Self-Transformation, Self-Observation and Metamorphosis. *J. Amer. Psychoanal. Assn.*, 11:173-223.

LOEWALD, H. (1962a), Internalization, Separation, Mourning, and the Superego. *Psychoanal. Quart.*, 31:483-504.

—— (1962b), The Superego and the Ego-Ideal. *Int. J. Psycho-Anal.*, 43:264-268.

LYND, H. M. (1958), *On Shame and the Search for Identity*. New York: Harcourt, Brace.

MAHLER, M. S. (1952), On Child Psychosis and Schizophrenia: Autistic and Symbiotic Infantile Psychoses. *The Psychoanalytic Study of the Child*, 7:286-305. New York: International Universities Press.

—— (1957), Problems of Identity. Abstracted in Panel: Problems of Identity, reported by D. L. Rubinfine, *J. Amer. Psychoanal. Assn.*, 6:131-142, 1958.

—— (1958), Autism and Symbiosis. Two Extreme Disturbances of Identity. *Int. J. Psycho-Anal.*, 39:77-83.

—— & ELKISCH, P. (1953), Some Observations on Disturbances of the Ego in a Case of Infantile Psychosis. *The Psychoanalytic Study of the Child*, 8:252-261. New York: International Universities Press.

—— & GOSLINER, B. (1955), On Symbiotic Child Psychoses. *The Psychoanalytic Study of the Child*, 10:195-212. New York: International Universities Press.

OLDEN, C. (1953), On Adult Empathy with Children. *The Psychoanalytic Study of the Child*, 8:111-126. New York: International Universities Press.

—— (1958), Notes on the Development of Empathy. *The Psychoanalytic Study of the Child*, 13:505-518. New York: International Universities Press.

PANEL: The Vicissitudes of Ego Development in Adolescence, reported by A. J. Solnit. *J. Amer. Psychoanal. Assn.*, 7:523-536, 1959.

PAVENSTEDT, E. (1956), The Effect of Extreme Passivity Imposed on a Boy in Early Childhood. *The Psychoanalytic Study of the Child*, 11:396-409. New York: International Universities Press.

PIAGET, J. (1936), *The Origins of Intelligence in Children*. New York: International Universities Press, 1955.

[223]

—— (1945), *Play, Dreams and Imitation in Childhood*. New York: Norton, 1962.

PIERS, G. & SINGER, M. (1953), *Shame and Guilt*. Springfield, Ill.: Thomas.

PROVENCE, S. & RITVO, S. (1961), Effects of Deprivation on Institutionalized Infants: Disturbances in Development of Relationship to Inanimate Objects. *The Psychoanalytic Study of the Child,* 16:189-205. New York: International Universities Press.

RAPAPORT, D. (1956), Personal communication.

—— (1958), The Theory of Ego Autonomy: A Generalization. *Bull. Menninger Clin.,* 22:13-35.

REICH, A. (1953), Narcissistic Object Choice in Women. *J. Amer. Psychoanal. Assn.,* 1:22-44.

—— (1954), Early Identifications as Archaic Elements in the Superego. *J. Amer. Psychoanal. Assn.,* 2:218-238.

—— (1960), Pathological Forms of Self-Esteem Regulation. *The Psychoanalytic Study of the Child,* 15:215-232. New York: International Universities Press.

RITVO, S. & SOLNIT, A. J. (1958), Influences of Early Mother-Child Interaction on Identification Processes. *The Psychoanalytic Study of the Child,* 13:64-85. New York: International Universities Press.

—— —— (1960), The Relationship of Early Ego Identifications to Superego Formation. *Int. J. Psycho-Anal.,* 41:295-300.

ROCHLIN, G. (1959), The Loss Complex. *J. Amer. Psychoanal. Assn.,* 7:299-316.

ROOT, N. (1957), A Neurosis in Adolescence. *The Psychoanalytic Study of the Child,* 12:320-334. New York: International Universities Press.

SACHS, H. (1928), One of the Motive Factors in the Formation of the Superego in Women. *Int. J. Psycho-Anal.,* 10:39-50, 1929.

SADGER, J. (1911), Haut-, Schleimhaut- und Muskelerotik. *Jb. Psychoanal. Forsch.,* 3:525-556.

SANDLER, J. (1960), On the Concept of the Superego. *The Psychoanalytic Study of the Child,* 15:128-162. New York: International Universities Press.

SARLIN, C. N. (1963), Feminine Identity. *J. Amer. Psychoanal. Assn.,* 11:790-816.

SAUL, L. J. (1960), *Emotional Maturity*. Philadelphia: Lippincott.

SCHAFER, R. (1960), The Loving and the Beloved Superego in Freud's Structural Theory. *The Psychoanalytic Study of the Child,* 15:163-188. New York: International Universities Press.

SCHILDER, P. (1936), Remarks on the Psychophysiology of the Skin. *Psychoanal. Rev.,* 23:274-285.

SCHUR, M. (1953), The Ego in Anxiety. In: *Drives, Affects, Behavior,* ed. R. M. Loewenstein. New York: International Universities Press, pp. 67-103.

―― (1955), Comments on the Metapsychology of Somatization. *The Psychoanalytic Study of the Child,* 10:119-164. New York: International Universities Press.

―― (1958), The Ego and the Id in Anxiety. *The Psychoanalytic Study of the Child,* 13:190-220. New York: International Universities Press.

―― (1960a), Discussion of Dr. John Bowlby's Paper. *The Psychoanalytic Study of the Child,* 15:63-84. New York: International Universities Press.

―― (1960b), Phylogenesis and Ontogenesis of Affect- and Structure-Formation and the Phenomenon of Repetition Compulsion. *Int. J. Psycho-Anal.,* 41:275-287.

SPIEGEL, L. A. (1951), A Review of Contributions to a Psychoanalytic Theory of Adolescence: Individual Aspects. *The Psychoanalytic Study of the Child,* 6:375-394. New York: International Universities Press.

―― (1958), Comments on the Psychoanalytic Psychology of Adolescence. *The Psychoanalytic Study of the Child,* 13:296-308. New York: International Universities Press.

―― (1959), The Self, the Sense of Self, and Perception. *The Psychoanalytic Study of the Child,* 14:81-109. New York: International Universities Press.

―― (1961), Disorder and Consolidation in Adolescence. *J. Amer. Psychoanal. Assn.,* 9:406-416.

SPITZ, R. A. (1953), Aggression: Its Role in the Development of Object Relations. In: *Drives, Affects, Behavior,* ed. R. M. Loewenstein. New York: International Universities Press, pp. 126-138.

―― (1955), The Primal Cavity. A Contribution to the Genesis of Perception and Its Role for Psychoanalytic Theory. *The Psychoanalytic Study of the Child,* 10:215-240. New York: International Universities Press.

―― (1957), *No and Yes: On the Genesis of Human Communication.* New York: International Universities Press.

―― (1958a), On the Genesis of Superego Components. *The Psychoanalytic Study of the Child,* 13:375-404. New York: International Universities Press.

―― (1958b), *Field Theory of Ego Formation and Its Implication for Pathology* [The Freud Anniversary Lecture Series, The New York Psychoanalytic Institute]. New York: International Universities Press.

[225]

BIBLIOGRAPHY

STERBA, R. (1942), *Introduction to the Psychoanalytic Theory of the Libido.* New York: Nervous and Mental Disease Monographs, No. 68.

TAUSK, V. (1919), Über die Entstehung des "Beeinflussungsapparates" in der Schizophrenie. *Int. Z. Psychoanal.,* 5:1-33.

WHEELIS, A. B. (1958), *The Quest for Identity.* New York: Norton.

WINNICOTT, D. W. (1953), Transitional Objects and Transitional Phenomena. *Int. J. Psycho-Anal.,* 34:1-9.

—— (1960), The Theory of the Parent-Infant Relationship. *Int. J. Psycho-Anal.,* 41:585-595.

Indexes

Name Index

Subject Index

Activity, 43-45, 74; *see also* Passivity
Acting out, 134, 203, 210-211
  in adolescence, 177-180
  sexual, 166-167
Adaptation, 29, 31, 140, 150, 172, 188
Adolescence, 138-143, 151, 170-193
  and superego development, 126-130,
    134-135
  compared to oedipal period, 170-
    171
  consolidation of personality, 75
  creativity in, 81, 185
  differences in sexual behavior of
    boys and girls in, 166-168
  disturbances of identity in, 24-25,
    28; *see also* Identity
  failure of conflict solution in, 197,
    200-216
  identity formation, xii-xiii, 25, 31-
    32, 140, 160-171
  reactivation of infantile conflicts,
    135
  regressive process in search for new
    object, 208-209
  revival of oedipal conflict in, 50.
    170-173
  role of ego and superego identifi-
    cations, 92

shame conflicts, 142-143
  see also Conflict
Affects
  and cathectic processes, 84-86, 132-
    134
  and discharge processes, 8-11, 84-
    86
  and mother-child relation, 42
  and superego, 130-131
  attached to ego functions, 53
  development, 52-55, 76, 125
  in adolescence, 159-169
  inhibition of, in sleep, 11
  precursors, 11
  primitive, 7
  psychophysiological forerunners of,
    10-11, 15
  resomatization, 11
  signals, 53-54
Aggression
  alternating with love, 44-45
  anal, 99-100
  and depression, 84, 99, 189
  and devaluation of object, 105-108
  and ego interests, 78
  and guilt and shame, 146-155
  and idealization, 109-118
  and identification, 65, 93-94

[231]